AUBYN THOMAS

CUSTOMER INSPIRED MARKETING

Change the game and become the brand they REALLY love

AuthorHouse™
1663 Liberty Drive
Bloomington, IN 47403
www.authorhouse.com
Phone: 1-800-839-8640

© 2009 Aubyn Thomas. All rights reserved.

No part of this book may be reproduced, stored in a retrieval system, or transmitted by any means without the written permission of the author.

First published by AuthorHouse 9/14/2009

ISBN: 978-1-4490-0500-9 (e)
ISBN: 978-1-4490-0499-6 (sc)
ISBN: 978-1-4490-0498-9 (hc)

Printed in the United States of America
Bloomington, Indiana

This book is printed on acid-free paper.

For Mom and Dad.

Thanks for being at the root of my inspiration and for helping me every step of my journey.

A Refreshing New Approach to Becoming the Brand They LOVE

Marketing to customers in today's environment is an intense challenge. Hundreds of thousands of new products are launched each year, channel evolution is occurring at light speed and customer preferences are less predictable. Companies in the US spend more than $150 billion dollars in marketing and advertising today, – creating a LOT of noise in the system.

To add to these trends, your customer is DISTRACTED! They are only placing tiny fragments of attention thousands of places each day. Today's world of

- Instant Messaging
- Saturated sensationalism
- Hyper markets
- Information at warp speed
- Immediate gratification
- Ubiquity of presence – messages *everywhere*
- Multi-tasking
- Professional over-exuberance
- Virtual expressionism

It's no wonder that it is so difficult to achieve that sense of CONNECTION to their passions and deliver products and services they truly value! Many companies are experiencing diminishing returns on their marketing investments as they try to compete in an ever-complex media and channel environment. Are you one of them? Are you placing your bets in the right place for creating a winning relationship with your customers?

Customer marketing strategies need to constitute the essence of the company's DNA and must address areas of true interest and passion for its customers. I define it as customer inspired marketing and suggest that it best occurs when the area of passion for the customer intersects the area of passion and strength for the company. By finding their own intersection-of-value, new sources of value are created, thus giving the company a leg up on making a powerful emotional connection with its audience that lasts.

Join the revolution for a new marketing mentality! Practices that are customer inspired and remain at the heart of what you do best will put you on the right path to live the brand every day.

I will introduce several insights that I call Customer Inspired Principles (CIP), throughout the book. I hope you find the steps and principles helpful and may you enjoy your journey!

Aubyn

Contents

Introduction 1

Chapter 1
The Customer 9

Chapter 2
Regrouping 19

Chapter 3
Building a Passion for the Customer Helps
Your Company Survive...27

Chapter 4
Step 1: Have an Inspired and Informed View
of Your Customer..39

Chapter 5
Step 2: Determine How Your Customer
Views You 53

Chapter 6
Step 3: Know What Your Customers Value
in a Relationship with You..69

Chapter 7
Step 4: Become Proactive 85

Chapter 8
Step 5: Attack the Causes of Mediocrity 101

Chapter 9
Step 6: Ignite the Power of People—Building
and Nurturing the Winning Culture 113

Chapter 10
Step 7: The Small-Business Owner: Overcoming
the Challenges of Limited Resources 123

Chapter 11
Step 8: Celebrate and Build for the Future 127

About the Author 135

Introduction

Whether you are in charge of brand marketing at a Fortune 100 company, or responsible for increasing sales at a four-person company, the goal is the same: to develop, propose, and sell the brand in a way that keeps customers in a happy, loyal relationship. Whether you refer to yourself as a brand marketer, a product line manager, an ad exec, a technical designer, or simply the owner, you face the same challenge: to find the best approach for managing your brand. Marketing demystified—it's more than a notion.

When brand marketers (a generic term I'll use to refer to all of the above) experience dramatic changes in the marketplace, as many of us have in the last two years, we often find ourselves second-guessing things and questioning the success of our current marketing methods. We are searching for more enlightened and effective ways for shaping the way we go to market. It's part of the natural evolution of business: growth, experimentation, discovery, and progression. Adversity creates an opportunity to ask important questions about improving our brands, including the following:

- What are the unique aspects of a brand that propel it into a coveted standing as the one people **really** want?

- How do some brands seem to effortlessly transcend the way people would normally think about them and become brands that capture an energized reaction from people?

- How do these brands catch on? Why is it that they catch on and have enduring value?

- How is it that these great brands make us think differently about life's simple endeavors such as buying a cup of coffee, doing an Internet search, buying a pair of shoes, or strolling through a local food market?

I believe these questions can be answered by following what I call the "observable truths" in brand marketing. These truths are little signals, like bread crumbs leading the way to success. We'll examine plenty of examples of transformational products that serve basic functions in life but that have become an experience that is sought after and desired—more a "way of life" than a mere consumer product.

These products, and the companies that have created and managed them, are constantly redefining the marketplace through the successful creation of value for both the company and the customer. It is happening even within a difficult economic climate.

In my observation, these achievements are met by creating an intersection between the passionate core of a company's operations and the passion of the customer. The passionate core is the "sweet spot" of a company's function, exhibited when it is providing the best of what it can offer in a way that employees comprehend and embrace. It's the end-to-end delivery of the company's ultimate purpose that aligns with the customer purpose.

This approach to branding takes it down the path to meet the customer's desire and activates connection with them. Companies are doing this well today, and across many different product and industry landscapes. By paying attention to the observable truths visible in the way these companies operate, we can all help our companies do a better job of capturing the magic that keeps our customers wanting more.

So what are some of these observable truths? In my view, the leaders of these groundbreaking companies have demonstrated a proven ability to build and highlight brand characteristics that anchor around an area of *passion*. Their reason for being is functional to the core of what matters to their target audience. At the right point in time. In the right way.

It's not just more of the same: it could be delivered through a new idea, or a new feature or version of an old idea that captures a customer's loyalty and passion. It's presented and positioned in a way that creates a spark that ignites something in them. They "get" what the company stands for, and they want to get behind it.

If you look at the signs that tell what a successful company stands for, you can usually see the existence of a signature theme or voice that announces the source of its strength and passion. You can see that in great companies, successful leaders have a drive or instinct that is a natural calling, a motivation that is in tune with an idea or vision that they've been able to embody at a very personal level.

These leaders have also successfully materialized that passion into a form of commercial worth. By doing so, they have built companies that experience terrific growth, resilience, and sustainability.

Of course, having passion and a calling is not nearly enough. Companies that have captured the imagination of the consumer have also transmitted their passion to their people. More important, they align their products and services to these shared areas of passion.

If a company's leadership can do these things, then magic occurs.

By understanding what inspires the customer and then finding that shared drive in a company's people, leaders are able to change the fabric of the company. This allows for the natural ability to present the product or service that the customer will embrace and gravitate toward—it is *customer inspired* and creates a much more relevant and meaningful engagement.

Introduction

The result? Demand follows and success is realized. By knowing the customer and this intimate affinity that they have, leading companies are able to channel their shared passion to form a more positive and valuable relationship. They are able to create an experience that allows them to do the best of what they do. And they bring the right people to the forefront to deliver on the promises they've made to the consumer.

Companies such as Apple have a demonstrated passion for innovation that successfully captures their customer's desire for individualism, expression, and fun. Their i-suite of products is integral to many people's lives today. These offerings permeate cultural awareness and acceptance and have become intuitively accepted as the "norm." The iPod and iTunes have become the common descriptive vernacular to define how music is accessed. It's not uncommon to hear someone presumptively ask a coworker or friend, "What's on your iPod?"

Ben & Jerry's Homemade Ice Cream operates their business in a way that reflects their passion for a more sustainable environment combined with a commitment to bringing the finest-quality, all-natural ice cream into people's lives. And they have made this statement publicly:

> We have a progressive, nonpartisan social mission that seeks to meet human needs and eliminate injustices in our local, national and international communities by integrating these concerns into our day-to-day business activities. Our focus is on children and families, the environment and sustainable agriculture on family farms.

This stated cause resonates and strikes a chord with what is on consumers' minds today and reflects their beliefs. Ben & Jerry's further exhibits its values through special events at the grassroots level, from the National Free Cone Day to the Election Elation celebration. The company is acting in a way that is true to its core values and reason for being in business, and having fun while doing it. That resonates. That works. Consumer acceptance is bound to evolve when a company puts an inspired passion into play.

Let's examine the compounding effects created by a passionate intention when brought to bear. Think about how you feel when you work on your passion, that thing you love, the project or the cause that when done right exemplifies the very best in you and how you want to define yourself. You know the feeling: you're excited, euphoric, enthusiastic, willing to work longer and harder, and able to draw energy from forces around you that you never knew existed. Time flies and more output is realized than you ever thought possible.

You can't wait to work on it and wish other things would get out of your way so that you could spend time on your passion. You are rich and abundant with ideas and creativity and there's an overflow of positive feelings; your output is prolific, and you often don't know why.

I suggest that this is because it is your calling and is directly tapped into an instinctive strength that is part of your DNA. You know that you are on to something and realize that you should try to do more to cultivate this strength. Unfortunately in today's world, many things distract us from doing so. It is unfortunate, because the more we can spend our time and energy tapping into our passions, the better we feel.

It's the same in the business world.

I have personally witnessed how this dynamic can exist and be cultivated in a productive and profitable way in companies, and it's fascinating to see. I want you to be able to tap into and leverage the passion and strength in your business through truly inspired customer relationships, and to create a more fulfilling working environment for your company as a result.

However, I do realize that it will be a difficult journey. It requires a bold, courageous approach at times. It means pursuing a new vision with a pioneering spirit and helping others see the value in this vision. Your passion is what will show you the way.

> "A strong passion for any object will ensure success, for the desire for the end will point out the means."
>
> *William Hazlitt*

Introduction

I have spent more than twenty-five years in Fortune 100 companies and have had the pleasure of serving in various marketing leadership capacities in industries such as hospitality and gaming, packaged goods, personal electronics, financial services, and retail. One thing that I continue to observe is the challenge that large corporations face with brand strength, customer intimacy, and employee engagement.

These corporations are unavoidably guilty of doing too much for too many, or the same thing for everyone, or not enough for those who matter most. Two key problems exist: First, maintaining the inner, personal knowledge of what motivates customers—especially given the fickle, insular, and skeptical nature with which they interact with companies today. And second, identifying and tapping into what gets, and keeps, employees charged up so that they can meet the challenge. How do you keep them functioning at their best in what they love to do so that the company's activities flow right into the sweet spot for the customer?

It is this business dynamic that is the focus of this book.

Why is this important? Because you must move customers from thinking that you have something that they simply *need* to something that they truly *want*. Needs-based thinking puts customers in a functional mind-set, and doing business with you becomes simply common or even commoditized. When they operate from a place of passion, their deep desire for a life-changing product emerges and the opportunity for growth is realized.

Take a moment to think about some of the most notable and iconic brands in our world today. Consider, for example, the brands that realize the highest rankings in the widely recognized annual study called the Interbrand study of the world's top one hundred brands (Best Global Brands, www.Interbrand.com). How did these brands achieve and maintain top ranking, and how do passion and customer intimacy play a role?

McDonald's focused on building better goodwill for their brand through healthier menu options. Prada kept pushing the envelope of edginess and taking fashion tastes into new territories. Kellogg's kept a good balance and brand visibility for both healthy cereals (Special K brand)

and things kids still really want (Pop-Tarts). Adidas jumped into new sponsorship relationships (the World Cup) that spoke to the heart of their consumers and kept them in a place where normally their competitor Nike would play. Starbucks continued its grassroots, community experience and stuck to its "nonadvertising"-based strategy. Motorola evolved from a technical company to one focused on customer experiences and being more integral in their customers' lifestyles (success of the Razr phone). Google continued to evolve and diversify its business offerings. BP continued to build equity in people's minds as being a provider of energy solutions that respect global environmental interests.

These are good examples that we can all relate to, but they beg the question: what are you and your brand doing today that creates strength, superiority, and meaning for your customer? How do your collective passions connect?

I am actually optimistic about how this phase of our economy will affect marketers' capabilities in general. I believe the economic slowdown will force marketers to get back to the basics, to function on a more transparent, bare-bones level, and to reestablish our fundamentals in ways that customers will understand.

We as brand marketers need to clean up the waste inherent in the superficial programs we've operated for years, programs that aren't adding any value to the marketplace. We need to focus on what can be done to create the most value for our customers in a way that is core to who we are.

I suggest that over the last ten years, we have come to a place lacking honesty, truism, purpose, and authenticity in business. The good news is that not all companies are lost in this chasm. And more important, even companies that have lost their way can find it again.

It is my hope that no matter what your business circumstance is—whether you are in a small company, just starting out, or working in a large corporation—there will be valuable and applicable lessons to be found in

Introduction

the examination of companies that have found a way to have their own passions intersect with those of the customer.

In the following chapters, you'll learn how you can build this capability into your own company, following just eight key steps.

During my years of marketing experience, I have developed a curiosity that compels me to explore the relationship between company and customer. I have led major business marketing organizations and built customer platforms, run multibillion-dollar businesses, and embarked on entrepreneurial ventures.

I have met and observed many different business practices, analyzed tactics and techniques, studied trends, and analyzed results. And yet, creating that bridge between customer and company still remains elusive. But with the help of this book, you'll be able to do it.

Chapter 1
The Customer

Every business, no matter what their product or service, is dependent on customers feeling comfortable with the company and their offerings. Whether that comfort comes from pricing, functionality, style, or customer support, the customer must reach an alignment with the brand to spend money supporting it.

The understanding of the critical drivers in the decision-making process pushes marketers to the edges of sanity: how to convince the customer that one brand is not only superior to another, but actually fits within their lifestyle and modality of thinking? The answer is highly subjective.

The consumer may enter into this decision-making process with extreme or drastic associations tied to an organization. They may think of the product as a mandatory source of well-deserved gratification (a bottle of wine) or attach life-crucial preservation requirements (a fire extinguisher). *Why* they buy is up to them and is subject to many different interpretations. And their inspiration may or may not be intuitive. Consider some of the inherent motivations that may affect the psychological approach toward a purchase decision:

1. Safety—"I need this Volvo because it's the safest car on the road."

2. Personal Validation—"I want this water filtration system because it confirms my commitment to the environment."

3. Physical Survival—"We must buy these flashlights and batteries in case of home or weather emergency."

4. Health and Well-being—"I will order a salad at this fast-food restaurant instead of the cheeseburger."

5. Joy or Fulfillment—"This software product will help start my home-based business and allow me to pursue my dreams."

6. Resolution to an Important Quandary—"I will buy more fruit as a snack substitute for my kids. They need to be ready to sit down as a family at dinnertime and eat a solid meal."

7. Expression or as a Personal Statement—"This new outfit will help me showcase my new status as a supervising professional."

When a purchase carries a personal and meaningful intention such as these, consumers seek a strong source of "relateability." They need to connect to a product offering in a *relevant* way, and therein lies the task before us.

Any discussion of how to build that connection, especially the kind we're trying to build—one based on shared value and passion—must begin with an understanding of the customer. We must first examine how we think about the customers and consider the motivations of their decision-making.

One thing is clear: *All customers have an ultimate purpose or desire that sparks a special interest in the goods or services that they buy:* to look youthful, to have cutting-edge technology, to get the best deal, to have the smartest kids, to be efficient, to protect their finances, to capture memories, to have recreational outlets, to be entertained, and so on. What is important is to be able to recognize these areas of inspiration and to be able to tap into them through your product, message, and experience.

> ***Customer Inspired Principle (CIP)***
>
> ***The goal for your brand:** get your customers away from the "functional" way of viewing your product. Take your brand to a place where more "emotion" is involved.*
>
> ***The situation at hand:** You believe that you already have created a compelling product or service that is ready to fill a need. You seek to better understand the source or inspiration for the need and how it might be changing for your consumer. How will you do this? By gaining a deeper understanding of the way your product enhances their lives and serves to advance what matters most to them.*

Finding that emotional connection, and then mating it to a common ground within your organization, will create space for you where the consumer wants to play.

The customer's engagement with the product or service should be an experience that is "as anticipated," intuitive, and satisfying. That means when the customer is being courted by a brand, they should not feel forced into a decision or be stressfully persuaded through intimidation as is so common in today's buying experience. It sets up the relationship for an anxiety-filled premise.

Does it really make sense to introduce high-pressure negotiations or manipulative sales tactics when you're trying to truly connect with a customer and to set the stage for an engagement that finds their passionate place? What customers really want is to naturally and easily expand on their interests, satisfy curiosities, do themselves proud, and align the purchase with their own objectives in a personal way—on their own terms.

Chapter 1

In an economy like today's, that can seem maddening to a marketer. We need sales right now! We can't afford to wait, because we may not be in business tomorrow!

But consumers are *also* wary. Many are losing their jobs and homes and facing circumstances that almost certainly cause them to revert to the brands with which they most identify. They will spend their money only where they feel comfortable and valued, and only for the items and services for which they are passionate. Think about how companies operate from a place of fear and intimidation in their engagement with customers today. How prevalent it is. It seems the more desperate sales and marketers become, the more they revert to these techniques and gimmicks. These scare tactics invoke a reactionary, panic-stricken response in the customer that is far from enjoyable because it feels more like a necessity than a desire.

I submit that this does not engender goodwill, passion, or a favorable state of mind in the customer. Not at all. When a customer sees aggressive language that follows the "buy now or else" methodology, the reaction is not one of connecting on common ground. Below are a few simplified examples of what I mean:

- You better buy now. Limited time only. You might miss out on the chance of a lifetime!

- Buy this or else you will suffer. Your family will be exposed to toxic germs in your kitchen!

- You look like a fool compared with others who buy this static-cling-removal product.

- We realize you don't have the intelligence to handle this problem yourself, so let us solve it for you.

- This is the only place this best deal is available.

- We have been around the longest; those other guys don't know what they are doing and will rip you off.

- Cheap imitations can't compare to our quality—we have the only product with real quality. Don't be fooled.

Scary stuff—but permeating the airwaves every day. The added pressure comes if you as the customer have the perception that you have only *one chance* to decide what to buy because your dollars are limited. What if I make the wrong decision?

As a marketer, I understand very well the need for "call to action" tactics and methods for differentiating from the competition. I understand that you feel that you have to shout from the rooftops sometimes to get anyone to take notice. I understand how it feels to try the "softer side of sales" and feel like you may be at risk of your audience ignoring you. Understand, I am not speaking of toning down your message or the actions you take toward satisfying your company's desire for more business. I am speaking of thoughtfully showing your customer that you know them and relate to them in a meaningful way.

You want to imprint your point of difference in a way that breaks through to consumers in a very crowded world of sales and advertising messages. I get that. But I also suggest that you are paying a price for aggressive practices and that there are more benefits to be had through reaching an *inspirational* place with your customer.

Defining inspiration as it pertains to your business is sometimes difficult. What does it mean for you to inspire the customer?

> ### *Customer Inspired Principle (CIP)*
>
> ***An* inspirational exchange *for your brand involves creating a positive attachment and creating an emotional basis of reference, and provides expected (and sometimes surprising) methods of gratification.***

Chapter 1

We'll get into that in more detail later in the book, but for now I recommend that negative forms of engagement be used sparingly and cautiously.

> ***Customer Inspired Principle (CIP)***
>
> ***When you operate from a fear-based method of coercion, you create a negative attachment that results in commoditization and indifference. Your customer does not care to have an intimate relationship with you or a flattering view of your brand because they see you as a means to an end. Create a win-win by working toward a place of inspiration for you both.***

In my years of experience as a marketer, I have learned a few things about consumers that I will bet you may have observed as well. One of those lessons relates to the consumers of today: they mainly operate in a mind-set that comes from being overstimulated and time starved, and they use a passive observation of communications that are exposed through a highly repetitive process. Their every moment of existence is intruded upon by a marketer trying desperately to capture a moment of attention. It's not only interruption but also intrusion marketing.

Consumers are weary from this bombardment, just as you are—and they have developed tools and weapons to defend themselves. I would guess that if today's consumers had a representative who could address the marketers invading their lives, they would say something like the following:

> I'm not listening. I hear you, but I am not really listening. Unless you show me that you understand more about my interests and needs and you intrigue me, you will never be able to reach me. I am in control and have little patience. I can eliminate your message, fast-forward through it, and push you out to oblivion with the click of a button. I can selectively block you from calling. I am smart and savvy, and I know how you are trying to insinuate your way into my life. What I hear is that you just want something from me, and you are not very knowledgeable,

convincing, or heartfelt. Brands instigate their way into places every day. It's obvious and forced. I simply process them through my filter, letting only what matters pass through. The brands that I enjoy, am loyal to, and respond to know me and talk to me in a voice that I want to hear.

Sincerely,

Your customer

The viewpoint of the customer seems more at odds with the viewpoint of the marketer than ever. Advertisements are harassments, and there are companies like TiVo capitalizing on their ability to grant the customer a modicum of relief from the constant barrage of selling, selling, selling.

If you've studied marketing at all, you've probably heard that the average person sees more than seven thousand marketing messages every day. By the time we reach the age of sixty-six, each of us will have seen approximately two million television commercials. The author of *Buyology: Truth and Lies About Why We Buy*, Martin Lindstrom, has calculated that that total is equivalent to eight hours a day, seven days a week for six years straight!

The good news is that consumers are still spending money. Though spending is down, there are still brands to which consumers are loyal and supportive. It is those brands that you will learn to emulate in this book.

Where Is the Passion?

The first step in finding a passionate common ground between you and your customer is to realize that everyone has areas of energy and drive that are special and that illuminate like a beacon for them. The only question is, does your brand do that?

Not exactly sure where the passion is? Remember that you have many options! A source of passion could emerge from a good variety of places within your business: not only in just the product you sell, but also the "no nonsense" way you sell it, or through the helpful and empowered people who support it.

Passion can come from the unique service that your company provides, the unmatched experience you create, the way you communicate with your audience, your cutting-edge innovation, technology—there is a great variety of possibilities. Just remember, whatever your special proposition is, it must be a source of excellence (what you do *well*), it must be achieved through passion for your organization (what your employees *have heart for*), and it must speak to passion for your customer (what they *really want*).

Though our current discussion is about the consumer, a major part of finding a passionate common ground with said customer is actually having a place or practice of passion within your organization.

Creating a corporate culture that engages in the delivery of intentional relevance requires a lot of discipline and consistency. After all, it is being brought to life by your employees, who need to maintain the passion themselves. This can be especially challenging in an organization that experiences high employee turnover or that has experienced cutbacks and outsourcing. It is difficult, I know. But it is not impossible. And without finding a way to create that level of passion—a passion that can then be honed and targeted for the consumer—does your organization really have the employee involvement that produces great customer experiences?

The customer can tell when an employee is not engaged. They can feel it in every transaction and every contact point. In organizations where the work is part time and the wages are low, inspiring greater care and a higher-quality customer experience will be more difficult. Later in the book we'll go through some of the steps you can take to engender some of this passion.

The beauty is that everyone wins when you find this common ground, and your business will evolve favorably as a result. Your marketing style then becomes less about contrived sales pitches and more about providing something to people that you believe in and that they want, care about, are loyal to, and are willing to pay for. You create an experience that is about emotional characteristics that build confidence and trust.

I have led major business marketing organizations and built customer platforms, run multibillion-dollar businesses, and embarked on entrepreneurial ventures. I have met and observed many different business practices, analyzed tactics and techniques, studied trends, and analyzed results, and yet, creating that bridge between customer and company is still evolving and is somewhat mystifying and elusive. It's really difficult to get it "brand-right" for the customer.

Facing budgeting and resource constraints, it might seem impossible to create a passionate company culture, but it is not impossible.

There are dozens of stories of customer-inspired leaders who saw the big idea through a customer lens, identified a clear passion that they too were able to share, and were willing to embark on a journey into unknown territory that involved an enlightened and profitable business engagement. These businesses have notable achievements, performance credentials, and awards—but the common theme is the inspired passion that they share.

The key is to keep the customer at the center of everything that you do!

You are a person who has passions. You have feelings and attachments, and you identify with certain brands and companies because they make you feel comfortable. *You* are a consumer. So start thinking like one and try to approach marketing from the customer vantage point when you make all of your important customer-facing business decisions. For example, when creating a new product package: what would the customer think? New enrollment process: what would the customer think? New staffing model: same question. Ask it over and over—keeping the customer's needs and motivations at the core of your decisions. Keep yourself honest and remain true to your customer promise.

Your transformation will look like this:

Chapter 1

FROM	TO
A rational brand	An experiential brand
A functional product	A motivational product
Serving your customers	Serving your customers' passion
A company they are *aware* of	A company they *embrace*
Part of their to-do list	Part of their lives
A practical connection	An emotional connection

Summarized as a key lesson will be the importance of finding the intersection of value for you and your customer. Consider the illustrative view in the diagram that outlines the opportunity.

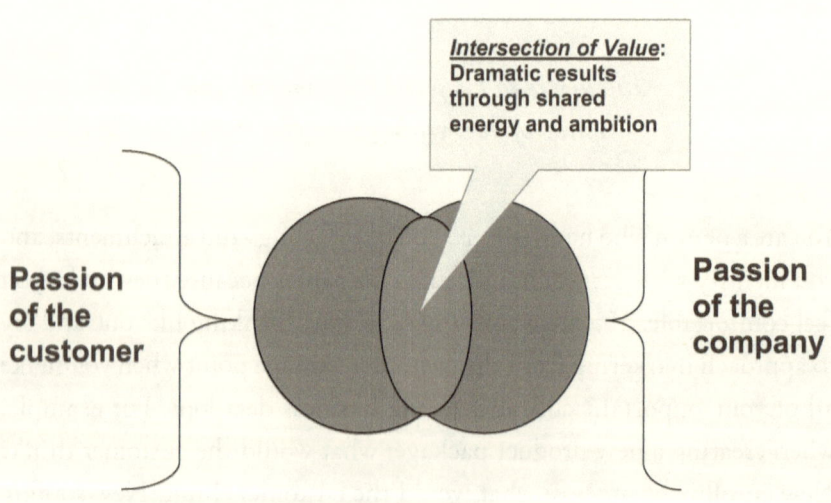

Where passion overlaps—opportunity

Chapter 2
Regrouping

The customer has changed. But so have marketers. We've arrived at a place as an industry where clever pitches, placements, and aggressive promotion tactics have supplanted an honest and relevant relationship with the customer.

It's time to regroup, reevaluate, rethink, and put some new concentration into the way we are marketing and selling products today. We have no choice but to press on in the pursuit of some new and game-changing ways for taking our brands to a higher level. Why?

Customers expect it. The competitive matrix requires it. Economic survival demands it. The old paradigm for customer engagement is becoming less and less effective, more imitated, and more redundant. We may have the right product for the right customer, but our ability to zero in on that magic rainbow that carries us into their minds and wallets is becoming more and more elusive. Innovation becomes mainstream. Trends quickly become obsolete. Practices are adopted on an accelerated curve. The viral effect creates instant access. Everything "now" is old news—including your product.

In spite of a crowded production economy, the proliferation of new products is not slowing down. It continues to add clutter to the market space and the consumer view. As new ideas emerge, the challenge for breakthrough acceptance grows more difficult. Even terrific ideas that appear to have marketability and promise face odds of success that are increasingly grim.

> *In consumer products, 75 percent of all new individual products fail. And according to the Global New Products Database (GNPD), the space is crowded: GNPD adds twenty thousand new products to its database every month!*

With so many products and business solutions out there for the customer, it is more challenging than ever to beat the odds and capture that source of true value that drives demand and profit. Nobody wants to be a failed statistic, which has led many marketers to embrace the aggressive, buy-now-or-else tactics discussed in Chapter 1.

As a business leader, or marketer, you see the possibilities in your organization. You have confidence in the potential to grow your business in exciting and innovative ways, ways that will connect with the passions in your customers. You see the potential on the horizon ready to be garnered through some of the following areas:

- Growth in business from existing customers
- Accelerated capture of new customers
- Better marketing and servicing models
- Improved employee engagement

You may know you have something great to offer that people want to buy, and yet the sales results you are currently achieving are not even scratching the surface of what you believe your potential is for growth. You might also be wrestling with the challenge of being able to get more return for every dollar that you spend because you can't afford waste.

If you're a marketer and don't have a say in what products or services are offered, then a line of communication needs to be established so that the product managers and product developers are seeing what you see.

If you realize that the customer is not passionate about what your organization does, no matter what your position is in the organization, raise a red flag and be a voice. Start by viewing it as your purpose to be an ambassador, an advocate for your consumer! We call this role the "customer champion," and it requires that someone be relentless in carrying the torch for customer realization and honesty.

The old methodology of building a fantastic product with the belief that a market can be developed for it just won't work. Connecting with a customer's area of passion means doing more than floating out a notion to the masses and hoping it sticks with someone.

You need to protect the integrity and reputation of your brand and yet be flexible enough to redefine it as market conditions change. You may see that you are losing a valuable share of your audience today and not have a clear vision about why because there are so many driving forces affecting the marketplace.

Oddly, the set of events that has brought us as marketers to our knees may also be our salvation. This humbling moment in our history should lead us all back to the basic principle that has been a recipe for success since the beginning of time: capturing a more intimate and personal relationship with those to whom you sell.

So What Now?

Decide what you stand for. What is your brand and why does your brand exist? What is your mission in offering what you do to the customer? Do you know?

Ideally, you're already thinking about what the customer really wants right now. I hope you're also thinking about what your organization's core passions and competencies are. If you are, then you're on your way to cutting through the overload of sensory input that customers face every day.

Chapter 2

I think about the number of e-mails that I read every day and wonder how I got to this speed of processing capability. I am sure you can relate. On any given normal business day I process more than one hundred e-mails and, skimming through, extract the pertinent information and respond. I get it done.

Many of your customers are living in the same accelerated fashion, processing messages, and unless it is something that they have passion for, they probably don't pay attention.

Given the light-speed nature of messaging today, it is more and more difficult to get someone to take notice, let alone carry them from light observation of your message to actual interest and desire for what you offer. To them it is just background noise. And they can't remember what you said anyway.

In *Buyology*, Lindstrom makes it all too clear that the way marketers are operating today just isn't cutting it. In 1965 customers had a 34 percent recall of the advertising that they were exposed to. In 1990, that number fell to 8 percent, and in recent history it was around 2 percent. And the author goes further, arguing that if you were asked who the sponsors of your favorite TV show—*CSI,* or *24*—are, you would be hard pressed to name even one. Except maybe *American Idol.* You can't help but notice those forever-obvious Coke cups on the judges' table.

The problem is that consumers hear things in an undifferentiated voice, tuning out what they don't need. Even if the message is somewhat relevant to them, customers know that another ad, offering, promise, or chance similar in nature will be along.

This attitude has been cultivated for two reasons: marketers are not effectively capturing their passion, and marketers don't have a demonstrated passion for what it is they are selling. That means you.

And yet even in this accelerated environment there are many points of interface that present opportunities for marketing to your customers. You are building a relationship with them through every point of contact, building impressions in many ways. There is your Web presence, your sales force, your product packaging, your prospecting, and so on. Your opportunities to reinforce your understanding of your customers and their passion is at each and every one of these interactions!

If you fail to capitalize on this, not only will you miss an opportunity to favorably build your brand, but the customer will feel the gap in service treatment. They are impatient and expect more—fast.

We Need to Start Being Honest Again

We are in an era of high customer skepticism and declining confidence, and earning trust and loyalty is more difficult than ever—especially when so many households are exercising such tight fiscal conservatism.

Consumers hold their own truths and values very closely, and continue to require consistent and convincing proof of a brand's ability to deliver on its promise. They want honesty and they are willing to reward it.

Demonstrating honesty is a task that falls onto every part of an organization. The sales force, the CEO, and the middle managers all must strive to create an honest interaction with the customer.

The job of the marketer is to demonstrate how that has permeated the company culture. And doing so is possible only if the organization has been honest with itself.

That may sound like the first part of a twelve-step plan, but as I said in Chapter 1, your best bet for creating a loyal following is to align your organization's passions with those of the customer. If the leaders in an organization aren't prepared to be honest with themselves about what their competencies are and what they have a passion for, they can never convey that message to the customer.

When Dave Thomas appeared in ads for Wendy's, the customer believed in what he said. He spoke directly to them, and his passion for his business was obvious. He didn't try to be Ronald McDonald or any other icon. He focused on his own passions and found a loyal following of people who felt the same way.

That approach is necessary now more than ever.

Customer expectations are gathered through a broad lens of influences that set standards very high. No longer are products evaluated within their defined competitive context; they are evaluated outside of their category, and customers hold you accountable for performance standards that mirror the "best of the best."

If you are in the restaurant business and have what you consider a specialized, unique, and localized offering that focuses on healthy cuisine, you have competition in places you can't imagine.

You are competing with specialty grocers like Trader Vic's or Whole Foods, traditional grocers who have ready-to-eat food products and salad bars, franchise restaurants like Applebee's with its "Healthy Heart" menu, and even McDonald's, which offers fresh fruit parfaits.

> ***CIP:** Delivering an award-winning experience for your customers now does not reside solely in the hands of any one entity within your organization. It is not just a marketing issue, or a sales issue, or a product or price construct. It really centers on the company's ability to galvanize valuable customer knowledge with the willingness and fortitude to strive for knowing the customers intimately.*

Valuing customers and striving to align their wants and needs with your brand is more important than ever. Often, companies are solely focused on the brand, which is often an outcome or symptom of an inward focus and not reflective of a necessary market-focused planning philosophy.

In the *Harvard Business Review*'s "Customer Centered Brand Management" (Rust, Zeithaml, and Lemon) the authors write the following:

> We know that to boost profits we must build customer equity by building loyalty and broadening our offerings to fulfill our customers emerging needs. But, though we "talk" customer

focus, we don't "walk" it. Instead we try and build brand equity assuming sales will follow.

The authors use General Motors' Oldsmobile brand as a good example of this phenomenon. Oldsmobile carried with it an image of being for fathers and grandfathers, and the audience for the brand was clearly growing older.

Attempting to recapture declining share, the company tried to reposition the brand by designing campaigns targeted at younger consumers. The goal was to make younger buyers aware of the brand and to attract them to the existing lineup instead of finding the right offering for them elsewhere in the GM portfolio or designing a new offering to meet their needs.

GM spent a substantial amount of money attempting to reinvigorate the brand but was unsuccessful, and Oldsmobile's market share declined from 6.9 percent in 1985 to 1.6 percent in 2000.

The company ultimately decided to discontinue the product line, and in 2004, the last Oldsmobile rolled off the assembly line in Lansing, Michigan, the same location where the brand was born more than a hundred years before.

Many diagnose the cause of the brand's demise as being poor leadership, a lack of investment, and so on. But one contributing factor cannot be ignored: they lost sight of who their core customer really was and why that customer bought from them in the first place. They did not have the right customer focus.

> ***Customer-inspired marketing as I define it simply means keeping the customer as the core focal point of all that you do and aligning that focus with your true passion.***

In subsequent chapters we'll examine case studies that demonstrate how successful a brand can be by doing just that. We'll also discuss how you can make that same alignment.

For now, though, a return to honesty is what's called for. I hope I've demonstrated how the marketplace has changed for us as marketers and

Chapter 2

that the methods we've developed to this point have led us away from what made marketing effective in the first place.

The consumer doesn't need your product or service, and they know it. They have myriad choices in the field, and they know how to find them. They want to spend their money with people they believe care, with people they believe have a vested interest in living up to their promises. Being that company means being honest within your ranks and with the customer.

You can build lasting customer relationships based on shared passion. Go to the next chapter and we'll start learning how.

Chapter 3
Building a Passion for the Customer Helps Your Company Survive

It's one thing for me to tell you that focusing on a shared passion is going to increase your business's potential for profits and longevity in the market. But you want more. You want proof. You want to see living, breathing examples in which the right source of value was created by the company and *dramatic* results were realized. So here it is.

There are several compelling business cases for the approach that we are discussing, and we will start by taking a look at some of the top performing companies in 2008: companies that had a demonstrated ability to withstand the pressures of the economic downturn while still driving growth and competitor superiority.

Procter & Gamble has been around since 1837, started by brothers-in-law James Gamble and William Procter. Today, the company is home to brands such as Crest and Tide, household names that draw customer loyalty like no other. So how do they do it after all these years?

Chapter 3

Let's begin with their stated purpose:

> We will provide branded products and services of superior quality and value that improve the lives of the world's consumers, now and for generations to come. As a result, consumers will reward us with leadership sales, profit and value creation, allowing our people, our shareholders and the communities in which we live and work to prosper.

Notice how the customer emphasis is evident in the language and commitment. The customer is a leading part of their culture, of their values, of their direction, and who they want to be.

Procter & Gamble have in essence said from the beginning that by improving the lives of their customers through superior value and quality, they will be rewarded with what every business wants: leadership sales and profit. But they've gone further and said that one of the rewards is value creation and the ability of the communities they work in to prosper.

That focus is one of shared passion. They have said to the world that they are a part of the communities they operate in and not just an organization bent on profit. They have built an image that says, "We care about you, and we'll show you that we care in the way we treat you, through the value in our products and the focus of our company."

That kind of image is one we all want, and it's one that is repeatable with the right focus and tactics.

This chapter can be seen as a continuation of the regrouping process, so I'm going to ask you a series of questions here to get the wheels in your head turning. These are food for thought, and they'll get you focusing on the need for a customer-centric approach.

- Are you putting the customer in the forefront in every facet of your business, and are you thinking very intelligently and specifically about *who* this customer is? Or are you putting your brand out in the broadest sense, treating everyone the same, paying for wasted efforts to reach those who are not and will never be receptive to your offer?

- Do you know who your best customers are and what their true passion is?

- How dependent are you on price versus total value-based equity? Do people know your brand and choose your brand primarily because of your price point relative to your competition?

- Have you put strategies in motion that will grow the customer experience and capture their passion? Do you think about the fact that the customer experience is *all encompassing*, involving every touch-point over time from the moment you are on their radar screen through repeat business?

- Are you acting solely in the "here and now" to drive immediate sales? Does this cause you to think more in the short term as it pertains to selling to your customers? Are you more *sales* focused than *relationship* focused?

- Can you isolate campaign effectiveness from overall brand health?

- You may see breakthrough or response to a particular campaign or "program of the day," but do you have the right things in place to grow the brand longitudinally—long term through sustained relationships?

Chapter 3

- Can you describe customer treatment processes that occur at every touch-point in your organization and how they are customer inspired?

- Do you recognize and treat customers uniquely and meaningfully?

- What are you doing to create memorable experiences for them?

- What do you do for your customer that might cause them to talk about your brand and recommend you to others?

The answers to these questions have a lot to do with the concept of you as the customer and the customer being at the center of your universe. You travel, you purchase, you order ... Are the companies that serve you meeting the criteria laid out in these questions?

Consider, for example a time when you may have experienced a world-class, surprising, delightful, and differentiating encounter with a company. I know, it doesn't seem to happen as often as we would like, but that just serves as further proof that if you can provide these experiences, you'll make customers for life.

When has a company been able to really step up and truly surprise and delight you because they touched an area of passion, energy, and importance for you? When did the experience actually break through the clutter of encounters that you have each day and cause you to pause and take notice, or even to smile? Did you tell someone else about it? What was the result? Do you seem to have a higher scale for evaluating excellence than you have in the past because of that experience? Many people do. It's the old "setting the bar" phenomenon, and it is happening all around you.

Here's an example:

I travel every week and have had more than my share of personal experiences with the travel and hospitality industry. I can easily speak to the many experiences of disappointment all travelers face and find it more difficult to call out the surprise-and-delight ones when asked. But there have been a few.

The truth is that when that one special, illuminating experience does occur, it really jumps out at you. For me, it creates an experience on an emotional level that can really keep me in a great place because I am invested. I have spent a lot of time and energy in the world of travel, so I seek experiences that are rewarding and comforting.

My personal investment and care and concern for that part of my life keeps it on my radar. I am emotionally attached at a deep and intuitive level and would enthusiastically engage with the companies that have created this feeling for me.

On one occasion, I was traveling to New York City for one of my many excursions there and was checking into a hotel that is a member of the Starwood family. I am a loyal member of their Starwood Preferred Guest program, so they have a basic knowledge of who I am. Well, it seems that over time, they have bothered to connect the dots and recognize my frequent travel patterns, so they've begun to leave little surprises and welcome gestures for me in my room upon arrival.

At first, they would leave little baskets with chocolate and pretzels and chips. Nice effort but NOT so great for the diet—a constant struggle for the road warrior that I am. After several stays, a hostess left me a card to fill out, and in the communication there was an inspired message speaking to her passion for excellence and creating world-class experiences for her customers.

What a coincidence! I have passion for a world-class experience when I travel because I do it so often, work hard, and want some little comforts whenever I can get them. I was happy to respond to her request to fill out a guest services card, and shared that one of my main interests in their facility was their fitness center.

Chapter 3

After that additional information was captured, the welcome baskets were healthy and felt like they were personalized just for me! Fresh fruit and a free pass to the fitness center upon my return awaited me. To any other guest, this may not mean anything, but to me it meant a great deal and went a long way toward solidifying my loyalty.

So what does an experience like this one tell you about Starwood and companies like them? Let's recapture how it's done right in the simplest terms:

- Know who your best customers are and identify how your shared passion can work to their benefit.

- Let them know that you know them and acknowledge your shared passion.

- Engage them in a way that is meaningful to them.

- It is a partnership, so ask something of them—in this example, they captured information about me that I was willing to give along the way, to make it that much more personal—which was worth it for me.

- Realize that building loyalty and customer profitability is a journey and must build over time across each and every touch-point.

- Create the culture of customer centricity and empower employees to act on valuable service opportunities. (More about this in the next chapter.)

As I continued my journey with that New York hotel, other little surprises occurred, such as the lobby staff knowing my name and greeting me when I arrived. There were surprise room upgrades, which made me feel like I was getting special treatment. The reality may have been different; the business may not have been full and there may not have been a trade-off or sacrifice from a profit perspective.

In reflection, you can see how this exchange—give-and-take scenario—worked. They knew the basics about me. They asked me to give them more information. I responded. They acted instantly and effectively. I was a happier customer and in turn, more loyal and profitable for them because I have been willing to pay a premium for their services.

So, I ask you to think about that differentiating experience that helped move you to a stronger opinion and loyalty to a brand. What were the things that caused you to find it so compelling? We will talk about some of those best practices and opportunities for you to help elevate your brand and products to a higher perceived value and thus achieve new heights in profit potential.

Gearing Up for the Future

Mylene Mangalindan wrote in *The Wall Street Journal* (April 2008) that interest in building customer experience capabilities will be high in the coming years. In a survey by Forrester Research, 91 percent of the 287 companies surveyed indicated that customer-experience technology would be an important priority in 2009. This trend is expected to continue.

Using these "customer-experience" tools, companies can better monitor customers and lower customer-service costs by promoting do-it-yourself service through their Web sites. There is a savings opportunity as well because of the self-service benefit gained from sending people to a Web site rather than a call center.

US Airways recently invested in some customer-experience capability to help get customers to purchase online. They found that a customer passion in purchasing airline tickets consisted of simplicity, speed, and a seamless transaction. They were not delivering on it. They were able to eventually find some simple fixes for problems that were contributing to customers abandoning their Web site before purchase and were able to convert nearly 100 percent of those customers who had suffered from the identified problem (frequent flier number not being recognized).

Don't Confuse Attitude with Passion

Attitudes matter, but don't confuse customer attitude with customer passion. We are all observing the reality in today's market, because like our customers, we are all concerned about jobs and homes and business.

Consumers are overwhelmed by the sheer volume of negative economic trends affecting them, and even households that enjoy a higher level of affluence are dialing back spending and taking more of a wait-and-see attitude about purchases.

This means it is more difficult to tap into the consumer's area of passion and to capitalize on the intersection in today's environment.

Let's look at the retail industry, for example. I have had the good fortune to serve as a senior vice president in marketing for one of the nation's leading apparel retailers. I am a constant student of retail and spending pattern trends, so when we saw a precipitous decline in spending in the second half of 2008, I began to think about what might be different in these economic times compared with the past. This kind of sales slowdown had not been seen in retail history for more than twenty years.

The slowdown was unprecedented, because even in previous challenging times, women always had a passion for looking good and feeling good about themselves and their family's appearance. The products that we offered would be resilient during financial downturn because they were always viewed as a desired source of self-expression, and people have traditionally been passionate about that, as long as value is associated with it.

Today, however, premium luxury distributors are experiencing sales declines of 20 percent and higher. Here are some examples from 2008:

Neiman Marcus—down to prior year
Sacks—down to prior year
Nordstrom—down 22 percent
Bloomingdale's—down 21 percent

Even mid-tier retailers experienced declines:

JCPenney—down 12 percent
Macy's—down 8 percent

But, at the same time, Wal-Mart is up by 6 percent, which provides one example of how the mentality of purchasing decision-makers manifests itself today. There is clear evidence of a **value migration** that the country is experiencing. The consumer is receiving and speaking the language of value.

It will be not only important, but a business imperative for corporations to understand the changing landscape of public sentiment. Today's successful businesses will be cognizant and current in the understanding of these marketplace nuances and will adjust their business model to align their strengths with what the customer inspires.

> *CIP: During a time of value migration, if you don't want to have to compete solely on price, customer experience will be a critical point of distinction. Knowing the customer passion and bringing your own passion to the table will be key.*

Another way of looking at this is to compartmentalize into two categories: Wants and Needs. In yesterday's more exuberant economy, people put more of the luxuries on the list of "needs," and now just the essentials are viewed as needs. The customer is now saying, "If it is something I can do without, I would rather place my discretionary dollar elsewhere. Maybe I won't spend it at all—unless I have a unique and defined sense of passion for what I am buying. And that will be the only exception."

Chapter 3

Even companies that had focused on premium branding before the downturn are changing their stripes. In February 2009, Starbucks announced a new marketing strategy highlighting the fact that most of their menu items cost less than $4.

What was once positioned as an experiential, highly valued retailer with an aspirational element and widely held reputation for service superiority is now marketing *value*. Go figure.

The same goes for Lexus, who began running ads in 2009 promoting the virtues of a car that has value in what they call the "Seven Costs of Ownership," touting the fact that their cars, which are more expensive than parent company Toyota's offerings, are really a value because they don't cost a lot to maintain.

How does this state of evolving attitudes and behavior affect your business? You're probably experiencing the impact in your current sales trends and realize that there is a smaller pie that most households can draw from. That means you must compete in new and innovative ways to break through and sustain a leadership position. You can do it with the proper vision and tenacity to get there.

> ***CIP:*** *Customer-centric companies work to change the focus from reaching as many customers as possible to growing sales with fewer, more profitable ones and by making that emotional connection with them.*

Leading customer-focused companies know that when the interest of the customer and the company are aligned, the exchange will be perceived as a mutually beneficial experience. The company is better able to service the needs of the customer, and that feels good. They meet expectations, and customers are more likely to remain customers and have a higher willingness to recommend the product or services.

If you're like the rest of the business world, you are looking at ways your business performance is responding to the climate and concentrating all the best resources on what you hope will address the tightening discretionary spending. It is clear to you that you need to understand your customer more intimately than ever before, and you have most likely earmarked more than one customer-focused initiative into your short-term plans.

I have worked with several Fortune 500 companies to help them successfully grow their customer capabilities in a proprietary way that competitors could never exactly replicate. So how can I capture the essence of what our company cares about, its passion, and deliver that in a way that helps us get there? Let's go to the next chapter and find out.

Chapter 4
Step 1: Have an Inspired and Informed View of Your Customer

As business leaders, we have all examined the way we look at and value our universe of customers. How do you refer to them, describe them, categorize them, and prioritize them?

I have worked with several common architectures for classification over the years in various industries, and I've seen that there is no one right answer. It would be nice to have a set system of classification that could answer any questions we might have about which customers to target to make ourselves more money. Unfortunately, until that system comes along, we'll have to make do with actually getting to know our customers.

If you buy in to the core idea of this book, then I've convinced you that being more in tune with your customer is critical to the success of your company. Ideally that means you agree that how you "think" about the customer is also important. And you know that "one size fits all" won't get you nearly as much mileage as treating a customer with relevance and meaning can.

Combining these two ideas—a new way of thinking and a more precise classification system—is key for creating an in-depth picture of where your customers' passions lie. Doing so takes careful and deliberate attention, but if I can get you to embrace these concepts, I guarantee that

Chapter 4

you will move to a higher ground with your customers, which in turn will take you to new sources of profit.

How? Well, if you're like many brand marketers, you're most likely leaving money on the table because of a lack of recognition of people who *are* valued customers, or who *might be* valuable customers, or who are *at-risk* customers in need of reinvigoration. Don't worry—it's a situation even the best marketers find themselves in, and it's proof that effectively connecting with your customers is an ongoing process.

To start the process of reshaping how you view your customers, I'm going to ask you a series of questions designed to narrow how exactly you classify and rate your customers.

- How do you refer to and speak of your customer in your current environment?

- Do you use a "good," "better," "best" model?

- Are you mainly focused on acquiring new customers or growing the profit potential of existing customers?

- Do you think in terms of basic demographics? Such as "my best customer is age 35–49, earns $35,000 in average household income, is college educated, lives in a certain geography," and so on?

- When targeting businesses, do you think in terms of average revenue, number of employees, sales processes, vertical industries, business longevity, service territory, and other typical approaches?

The reason these questions are so important is that I want you to have some type of framework in place that has worked for you in driving sales volume. Based on that framework, I'm going to push you to think about applying a broader and more progressive view of classifying your customers to help exploit untapped opportunities.

To add more depth to customer classification, consider these areas:

- **Current Best Customers**—These customers may not be the highest spenders, or the most frequent purchasers of your product. They may exhibit other behaviors or loyalties that you should consider so that you're able to recognize and respond to them.

- **Potential Best Customers**—These customers may have a variety of characteristics for you to think about. They may be spending more with a competitor in the same category; why is that? They may be able to invest only a certain amount, but could potentially be given a reason to expand that spend.

- **Potential Lost Customers**—This category helps you keep an eye on attrition, the cause-and-effect rationale that helps you understand the drivers for why they are defectors or decliners. It gives you cause to put defenses in place to mitigate the loss.

When you start to engage in a deeper understanding within the classifications that work for you, it becomes possible to apply the "passion factor" to elevate your effectiveness. Think about how you can drastically improve your connection to your current, potential, or "at-risk" customers with the right delivery of what matters to them. Also think about how you can *customize* that delivery of passion for each audience. How can you make this connection in ways that align with your own organization's strengths so that it becomes natural, more productive, and maybe even fun?

Here's a simple example of where I want you to be when thinking about connecting with your customers:

I have a friend who is a family-practice physician in a rural community in Ohio. He has a small family practice that has had the benefit of enjoying many years of presence and service in his town. When I asked him how he classifies his customers or patients and targets them, he described the typical characteristics: age, family, geography, and so on. But what was interesting was that he thought he had recently tapped into a very simple yet successful approach to building a relationship with customers and bringing in new business.

By focusing on his own (somewhat obsessive, as he described it) passion for baseball, he found a new way to connect with people who shared the same passion. He decided to invest his small marketing budget, which he had historically used to run a little advertising now and then, in the sponsorship of a Little League team.

Because his sponsorship was an authentic extension of what mattered to him, it felt effortless to take the sponsorship to another level and actually show up and root for the team when he could. He did small favors for the team members and gave them a season-end victory pizza dinner to recognize their efforts.

The result of his involvement was a new way to look at how he spent his marketing dollars and how he could align those expenditures with his own passions. He came to think that his practice's presence and name on the uniforms was only the start, that he would like to continue his involvement with the team because he genuinely cared for them.

His enthusiasm and interest gave people a different picture of him, and he believes the relationships that grew as a result brought in more new business than his past local advertising program. Although his results may not carry with them the scientific data we as marketers like to rely on, his efforts have produced results that he can observe in person. He now thinks that a more involved approach is the right thing to do for a customer who shares his passion.

My friend is an example of someone who keeps the customer at the center of all business activities. Whether in a big or small company, the customer definition must be clear and aligned with the strength and passion of your company. It must remain at the *center* of all the organizational extremities.

Whether it is your Web site, your direct mail, your sponsorship choices, your employee programs, your selling approach, or any other facet—the experience must be orchestrated across every customer-facing transaction and remain true to the *Passion Intersection*.

Here's another example, on a larger scale:

McDonald's is a large organization that has established a culture built on the customer. They have implemented a state of mind that keeps the customer as the center of the company's focus. And they are also an example of an organization that understands the constant nature of adjustment and study needed to keep up with customer demands and interests.

McDonald's recently suffered from an increase in guest complaints and placed the quest for improvement in this arena at the center of focus in 2007. They were experiencing 20.1 complaints per 100 guests compared with 18.5 the year before and knew something had to be done, because as a recognized brand, their failures are public. In fact, Richard Gibson reported in *The Wall Street Journal* (February 2007) the myriad of problems that guests were experiencing, including these:

- Transaction accuracy—or the lack of it—accounted for about one-fourth of the more than five hundred thousand complaints logged by the company's customer contact center that year.

Chapter 4

- "Wrong item included in order" and "product missing" led the list of complaints, followed by "incorrectly prepared product," according to information e-mailed to franchisees and reviewed by Dow Jones Newswires.

- Other accuracy issues at which customers chafed included "condiments missing," "inadequate portion," customer "shortchanged or overcharged," and "napkins, straws or utensils missing."

- After accuracy problems, customers complained most about what they regarded as "rude or unprofessional" employees. Those gripes represented more than 15 percent of complaints.

- Speed of service was third, accounting for about 7 percent of complaints.

McDonald's management knows the passion their customers have associated with the McDonald's brand and that they expect speed, accuracy, fun for the family, and high-quality food. Failure to deliver on the customer passions would obviously lead to declining sales and damage to the brand.

Management took appropriate action with a broadly distributed report within the company designed to confront the problems directly and with accountability. They titled the report "Loud And Clear, The Voice Of The Customer" and reiterated that the company takes guest satisfaction seriously. One section of the report differentiates restaurants that it calls "brand builders"—those with the fewest complaints—from those with the worst record, which are labeled "brand destroyers." They even named in the report the managers who had winning and "need to improve" scores. It was a courageous but clearly visible and committed approach to improving the customer experience.

Not every organization would feel comfortable "calling out" their managers in such a way. But why not? If your organization is to connect with customers and share a given passion, then that passion has to exist in the employees who deal with the customers.

Retail food service is not an easy business to work in. Customers demand a high level of service at a very fast pace, and that is hard on managers and their employees. But it is the game McDonald's is in, so they must insist that their people reach for the stars when it comes to improving the customer experience.

Segmentation as a Strategy

How we classify or segment customers not only drives how we choose them, pursue them, and sell to them, but also informs the type of products that we offer, the service levels that are presented, the price points that are maintained, and virtually every other customer-facing function in our companies.

How brand managers think of, profile, and segment these customers is critical in every business environment that I have worked in. Sometimes a business is simply reacting to an emerging market space and finding that they have a real connection with the customers there.

Here are some examples:

- A leading financial services company—"We have seen a surge of Hispanic customers moving into our Sun Belt states. Maybe we need to offer a checking product that more specifically meets the needs of recent immigrants and have more marketing materials that speak to them in their language of choice."

- A multinational wireless provider—"Given the aging nature of the population, we should create a cell phone that is themed in historical cues like the Jitterbug and have big numbers on the device and a

- simple, low-cost service plan."
- Dunkin' Donuts recaptured a coffee-drinking audience after realizing that they did not need to imitate Starbucks to get a loyal base of less experiential and more purpose-driven consumers who are not caught up in the pretense of their leading competitor.
- Coach Designer Handbags recognized the power of the "new mom" segment and responded with a multipurpose diaper bag that offers a unique and attractive fashion alternative that brings style and elegance to a basic parenting function.

I have seen a lot of traditional approaches to customer segmentation in my experience, all pretty much using the same tactic. They look at age and household income and then prioritize based on the assessment of customer worth, meaning how much we think a customer is worth to the company. Perhaps you use this same approach in your business. It is a natural tendency, given the desire to identify and isolate those who spend the most with us, and it seems like an obvious method to use. The challenge is that this is typically done without emotional or attitudinal characteristics as part of our customer context.

To further illustrate this point, think about the people who look like you on the surface if you look at the basic demographic statistics. You may have a friend or colleague who is in your age range, lives in a similar geography, has the same family configuration, comparable income, maybe even the same amount of work experience or education.

On the surface, you two look exactly alike. But in reality you could not be more different as it pertains to the products you purchase, the brands you support, and the lifestyle you lead. Are companies missing out on this because they assume you are alike? How can they learn more about what inspires you and reaches you in that place of meaning?

Chapter 4

Part of the solution is to realize how important it is not to oversimplify how we characterize our customers. Consider the illustration below. It uses a typical linear approach to evaluating and prioritizing customers. It is a simple model in which a company might design marketing and target its customers. The $ value constitutes the priority in this case.

Typical Customer Segment Prioritization

Priority 1 - Spend level A
- Existing customers who spend most

Priority 2 – Spend level B
- Existing customers who spend less

Priority 3 – Spend level C
- Competitive Customers

Priority 4 – Spend level B
- Non-customers in the category, or lapsed customers

This figure may illustrate that you are thinking about customers differently based on how much they spend, but it is limited thinking. There are so many other ways to know and classify your customer beyond how much they spend with you. It begs the question, how could we add more perspective beyond this model to tap into the intersection of value?

A useful framework that I have been able to benefit from is the development of a multidimensional view of the customer's value. Through the implementation of an added lens with which to view and prioritize the customer, interesting things can happen.

Let's consider what some of these other filters might be for the purpose of making this point, keeping in mind that you will have to extrapolate the most important business-driving behaviors for your industry. You want to tap into areas of passion, interest, and relevance to the consumer and then make it part of how your company serves them. Here are some examples:

- Occasion based (how and when do they buy—events, holidays, life-stage occurrences)
- Value-based purchases (are they value seekers), cross-category purchasers (they like multiple things that you offer)
- Visitation frequency (they see you often)
- Peripheral category purchases (they buy related products)
- Lifestyle or affinity purchases (they are fans of something and like to belong as members, like Coach's "new mom" segment)
- High-volume purchasers (willing to buy in quantity)
- And the all-important multichannel designation for those who are willing to engage with you in more than one channel

And by adding these additional filters it is possible and feasible to garner insights about your customers relative to these other dimensions through a variety of ways.

You can learn what you need to learn about your customers through a detailed, formal research process, or take a more general approach that gets you there directionally. If you are thinking about taking on a customer-insights project to help get you closer to what matters to your customer, you need to be clear and up front about the objectives. You need to make sure your effort is thoughtfully planned and designed to get you the actionable data you need.

Whether you spend hundreds of thousands of dollars or a few hundred dollars, your objectives need to be clear and get you the outcome necessary to advance your customer-targeting methods. For example, you can analyze purchase history that yields both behavioral observation and reported data. This means that if you look at sales reports, you know from the transactions what was purchased. If you try self-reporting or "panel diaries" and have the consumer record what they are buying and when, you learn about your competitor's share of their wallet. If you match this with *some* insight into their other motivations, then you will be able to know something about a customer beyond what they spend. It then becomes a breakthrough opportunity for you because you will be able to readily identify ways to strengthen relationships once this information is leveraged. This information really can be powerful!

This powerful leverage comes from cross-referencing the worth-based stratification with the filter. We'll use brand affinity for this illustration. We know how much the customers are spending, and if we factor in those who purchased a certain amount of a particular product/brand, we're able to drill down more specifically into how to message to them, build products for them, and create more interesting and meaningful experiences.

Chapter 4

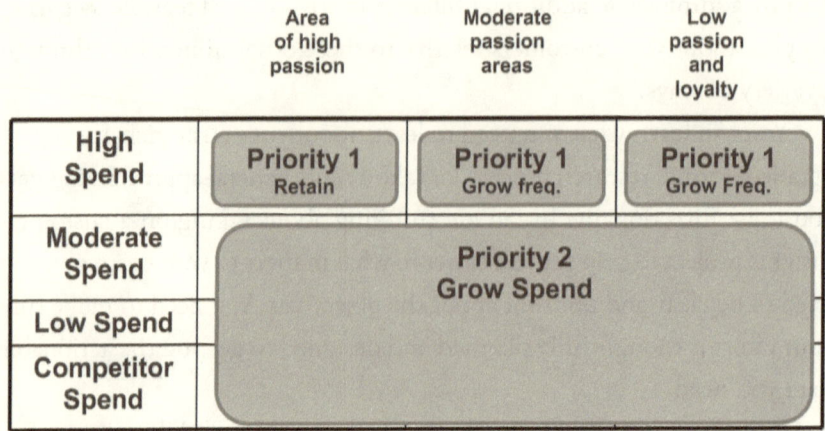

As you can see, by just adding a two-dimensional view you have created different ways to look at and think about the customer.

Let's look at an example.

During my work in the financial services industry, we were able to understand our customer's engagement and the depth of the relationship through a measure of balances—or more specifically, how much money was held in accounts with the bank. This is the typical "worth" segment approach that I have been speaking of. What was new at the time was an emerging method of analyzing customer value and opportunity for growth that was achieved **directly through their areas of passion:**

> **Customer Area of Passion:** Pride in family. Desire to see their family's next generation progress through advanced education.
>
> Business Opportunity: college savings products, loan products. *Be the partner in helping make their dreams come true for their children.*

Customer Area of Passion: career advancement through a new job position and relocation—moving for new opportunity, renewed optimism and hope for the future

> Business Opportunity: assistance with relocation to new banking center in new geographical area, home loan products, transfer assistance. *Be the partner at a critical and transformational time in their lives.*

Customer Area of Passion: planning for retirement, realizing the American dream of achieving the final stages of a fulfilling career

> Business Opportunity: investment services and client services. *Being the partner in their lives to help move them into being able to experience the best of all that they have been working for.*

These were actually chosen opportunities that were translated into major initiatives for the company. Why? Because the intersection-of-value was realized. We were able to find a core strength and purpose that the company was passionate about and present it as an answer to the customer's passionate desires. *A win-win!*

With this example that helps get you thinking about your environment, you are probably asking yourself, how can I act on this? Go to the next step to find out.

Chapter 5
Step 2: Determine How Your Customer Views You

Having an informed view of your customer is a great start toward implementing a new approach to marketing. Before proceeding to direct action, though, you need to layer on top of this knowledge an understanding of how your customers view you.

Although it might seem that having an informed view of your customer would encompass this concept, the reality is that it is its own category of knowledge. Customers today are more informed—some might say jaded—than they have ever been. Knowing their passions and demographics is essential, but we want to go further than that. We want to get "inside" their hearts and minds.

The customer's feelings toward your organization are what ultimately decides whether or not they will support you with their wallets, so the goal of course in developing an understanding of your customer's thinking is either to augment it or to change it. If your customer has a mostly positive view of your offerings and customer service, the opportunity is there to move them toward a shared passion. If consumers have a negative view of your company, there is more work to do, but still tremendous opportunity.

Chapter 5

To put the proper transformational levers in motion to get you to a higher-value position of equity and alignment with your customer, you first need a baseline reading. So let's take a look at your starting point.

Let me ask this question: what is your organization's current state—from a customer perspective? Let's do an audit of the important areas:

QUESTION: How do your customers view doing business with you and the experience they have in using your products today? What frame of reference do they impart in relation to your organization?

I once worked on a large financial services loyalty platform and quickly learned through consumer research that my audiences viewed the loyalty effort as a basic "functional" purpose; they saw the engagement as "transactional." Our customers viewed our marketing efforts from a very detached perspective, and didn't attribute any emotion to the process. To my audience, the marketing interventions we created were neutral; nothing about it was emotional or fun—let alone inspired. When we interviewed members about how they viewed our program and services, they would indicate that it "served a purpose but really didn't cause them to think more favorably about the brand." That's not good!!

ISSUE: *Do your current methods of brand involvement create an emotional connection with your valued customers? What influences does the price/value trade-off perpetuate?*

Without a branding message that creates some kind of emotional response, you will have left open a gap that keeps customers from ever reaching the "loyalty" phase in their view of your organization. Think about your own dealings as a consumer. There are brands you associate with feeling good, or with your passions and values, and then there are brands that serve only a functional purpose in your life.

Chapter 5

What brand of milk do you buy? Do you know? What about eggs, or celery? These products are widely viewed as being all the same: as long as the eggs aren't cracked and the milk isn't past its due date, consumers pay little attention to who the supplier is.

There are examples, though, of industries that have made successful attempts to overcome this perception by reaching out to consumers on shared ground. The milk industry is a fine example.

The "Got Milk?" ads have become iconic with the American public. So much so that parodies have cropped up on T-shirts, bumper stickers, and more. First aired in 1993, and paid for by the California Milk Processor Board, the first Got Milk? ad was a huge success, and spawned countless commercials touting the benefits of cow's milk.

The California Milk Processor Board was able to identify customer passions—health and well-being—and capitalize on that shared value. They touted the health benefits of milk, especially its high calcium levels, which they attributed as being beneficial to the health of bones and teeth—and who doesn't want healthy bones and teeth?

Notice that the California Milk Processor Board didn't identify a specific brand of milk producer. Most consumers are probably still unable to identify specific brands of milk producer because most producers are relatively local, and don't carry national recognition. Instead, the board focused on a national return to the consumption of cow's milk.

The expression "A rising tide lifts all boats" certainly applies in the case of the milk industry. By finding and focusing on the shared values and passions of potential consumers, the board contributed to an increase in milk sales in the United States. According to numbers compiled by the University of Wisconsin, the total milk and cream sales in the United States before the debut of the first Got Milk? ad were approximately 58 billion pounds, including sales of cream and flavored milk. Today that number has climbed to more than 62 billion pounds.

Although the ads themselves aren't the entire reason for the increase in milk sales, which may also be attributed to innovations in packaging (carry sizes, and so on), they are a great example of what can be accomplished when passions and values are aligned.

Chapter 5

But what about the people who sell the milk? In my experience in the retail industry, we have often observed that some distribution franchises are also viewed from a "utilitarian" perspective. For example, going to the grocery store, where they sell the milk, is usually viewed as a utilitarian exercise for consumers, but some retailers have made efforts to change that.

When you examine the aesthetic and environmental aspects of The Fresh Market and Whole Foods stores, you clearly see a world designed to transport the audience onto a unique and all-encompassing path of discovery and entertainment, through exercises such as wine tasting and specialty food samples. I don't know about you, but I always leave these stores with some impulse buys, which is just fine with them.

If your company is one that hasn't been able to conjure an emotional reaction when your customers interact with it, as the milk industry and some of their distribution franchises have, then customer education may be the bedrock on which you can build a new relationship. The important question to ask is this one:

QUESTION: How aware are your customers of the core benefits of doing business with you? Do they know what's in it for them? How can they see the inspired strength of your business—how can you make it more evident that to be a long-term, deeply entrenched customer is just what they need?

POSSIBLE ISSUES: *You have great reasons for them to try you and be loyal members with you, but they are not aware of those reasons. That means you have a good-value proposition, but it is not translating in the marketplace. Only those who are already your best customers are clued in to this little treasure, but how much are they talking about it?*

Consider Harley-Davidson, for example. Most brand followers are aware of the strong sense of passion, advocacy, and community that Harley owners share. The company does a wonderful job of delivering on their promise of a passionate experience because the company's workers and leadership embrace and embody the passions of the consumer.

To illustrate their commitment to the consumer, Harley-Davidson has successfully created a loyalty program that delivers on a unique and meaningful promise for its valued members: the Harley Owners Group (H.O.G). How does it work?

Through a paid membership (additional revenue stream—another plus), Harley offers its owners the opportunity to connect and share in a common purpose: the enjoyment of owning a Harley-Davidson and the chance to meet other owners.

Members of H.O.G are rewarded for their participation in club-related events through a series of rewards, including the following:

- *HOG Magazine* subscription
- *HOG Tales* newsletter
- E-mail updates on apparel specials, upcoming rides, and so on
- Fly and Ride program
- VIP treatment at certain events
- Roadside assistance
- HOG Travel Center for help with discounted travel accommodations

By pursuing a service level not shared by other manufacturers, Harley-Davidson has sought to earn the loyalty of its customers by going beyond just the purchasing experience. They have made efforts to build relationships with their owners long after the owners have left the dealership for the first time.

Chapter 5

The good news is that Harley's customers seem to be aware of what a relationship with the brand can bring, and the owners' club has been cited as a leading draw toward purchase intent. Motorcycle riders who are considering the purchase of a motorcycle are responding to Harley's commitment to their lifestyle, which is their passion.

What Harley-Davidson has done is show the importance of understanding what kind of product you sell. If your product is a disposable one that is simply utilitarian, your approach to building customer loyalty will be different from a motorcycle company's. Find ways to go beyond the initial purchase experience and you will find ways to build loyalty.

If the consumer is not aware of the value proposition inherent in your product, as it is in the case of Harley-Davidson, efforts need to be made to create more visibility for your product. Consumers need to be shown what is good and customer-forward in your offering. Harley Davidson captures the "heart" of what's best about being a member and allows customers to share in the heart of what they cherish about the brand. Ask yourself this:

> *QUESTION: What is the perceived difference between engaging in a relationship with your company and engaging with your competitors? Remember, I am talking specifically about not just the product or service that you sell, but going beyond that. What do consumers think more broadly about the whole experience of being in a relationship with your brand? The term relationship implies customer knowledge, demonstrated support, and familiarity. It also implies reciprocity. Are you perceived as being "like all the rest"?*

> **POSSIBLE ISSUES: Most good ideas are copied; developing a breakthrough service-delivery system that is proprietary and sustainable is difficult in today's marketplace. When your company successfully carves out that space, you insulate your customers from the competition.**

58 *Aubyn Thomas*

Chapter 5

Much as competitors try, they have not been successful in an effective replication of the Starbucks experience—from the perspective of those true, unyielding loyalists who don't believe that any viable substitute exists. Perhaps you know someone who will walk the extra four blocks to get the real thing and cannot accept imitation without tremendous resistance. Perhaps you are that person.

Creating the "unique" in the business world is never easy. It can seem impossible when you share a competitive field with companies that are pursuing the same technologies you are. But is it really the technology that sells your products in the first place? If you sell coffee, as Starbucks does, is it really impossible for competitors to make coffee that is as good?

What consumers crave is the ability to identify with a brand, to have a routine that involves brands they feel comfortable with. Starbucks has been able to build that identity and create a place where their customers are insulated from believing that any other brand can offer the same combination of product and experience.

Apple is another example of a company that offers more than just a "product." Apple's platform defines and exploits the wave of individualism and self-expression seen in their products and marketing. It is another example of a uniquely defined engagement, from product to communication to service delivery, and is indicative of their core proposition. And most important: it works.

If you've answered some of the above questions and found your organization lacking in the way that it pursues a meaningful exchange with consumers, then perhaps you have thought about changing. Change in the business world is a requirement for survival, but some organizations are better equipped to handle it than others. Which leads to this question:

> *QUESTION: What is your organizational readiness for change? Are you skilled and nimble enough to respond to the changing customer landscape as you prioritize it more strategically? How well can you assess and mitigate risk?*

Chapter 5

> ***POSSIBLE ISSUE:*** *Many operational and economic barriers will stand between you and your new customer-centric delivery system. It will be a daunting task to overcome them.*

Best Buy recently faced some critical decisions around how to better capture and enroll loyal members in their relationship program. They asked themselves how a nationally distributed retailer with more than a thousand stores and more than a hundred thousand employees could achieve a valued relationship with their customers.

Best Buy had seen the strength of what their loyal customers could bring to their bottom line, so they sought to increase the number of customers who would choose Best Buy first. Their motivation was obvious: Best Buy has enjoyed a sales performance from those in their program that is more than double that of consumers who are not.

So who were these loyal costumers, and how could Best Buy find more of them? In my experience, loyal customers share several common attributes regardless of the type of company or even industry. Consistent with most other companies that I have studied, Best Buy loyal customers meet the highly sought-after criteria of demonstrated attributes:

- Loyal customers in their program and in a relationship are less inclined to have complaints or rate low satisfaction scores—they are generally happier partners with the brand.

- They are less inclined to defect.

- They are less receptive to competitive offers.

- They stay longer.

- They are easier to service and are a lower drag on service costs.

- They are more likely to cross-shop.

Unfortunately, customers like these are not always willing to step forward on their own. Sometimes it takes a little coaxing to bring the best customer into a relationship, even one that is mutually beneficial.

Best Buy originally had a fee-based program. Their valued customers would pay a small price to join the rewards program and in return were part of an exclusive club. Only those with a strong enough affinity with the company would be willing to join and invest, but if they did, they became part of a special population.

The fee-based structure worked well enough, but eventually the number of new entrants into the program began to slow down because of a limited universe of potential members. Best Buy's vice chairman and CEO, Brad Anderson, clearly recognized the value of relationships and building a customer-centric organization, so in 2004, he put a stake in the ground and empowered a companywide focus on customer-centricity.

Anderson envisioned the organization striving to unlock the door to deeper relationships with their customers through solutions and services delivered through the Web, stores, call centers, and in-home services, and charged the program with taking a leading role in the integration of everything the brand has to offer.

The marketing team, in partnership with key agency contributors, built the infrastructure for a new relationship offering that eliminated the entry fee for the customer and mitigated costs that would have eroded margin by restructuring the benefit architecture. Some new methods for rewarding customers were introduced and they offered more flexibility and choice. Customers had better access to information that was relevant to them. For example, if you made a purchase in home electronics – a flat panel tv, for example – you would have access to mailers and web content that spoke to other products and services that related to the TV: home theatre, equipment (digital camera) integration and tips for a better in-home experience. People flocked to join (membership tripled from 2006 to 24 million members in 2007!) How was this achieved?

The new customers who joined the membership program "got it." They perceived that the value proposition was clearly communicated at all touch-points and that their loyal behavior would be rewarded. That may seem like a simple process, but as a leader over these types of initiatives, I realize that it is a major effort that requires multifunctional collaboration. Systems, marketing, data repository, legal, merchandising, human resources (employee incentives or not …) all have to play nice in the sandbox.

Despite the difficulty of implementing a program like Best Buy's, the process is made infinitely easier when there is a commitment from the top. Senior management must have the willingness to embrace a significant investment in the customer as the future. I submit that that commitment makes for a winning formula.

Overcoming Negative Perceptions

You are probably aware of the adage that says that for every one customer who vocally complains about a service or product, there are probably ten other people who felt the same way and didn't bother responding to a survey. In the case of large-scale marketing, those numbers grow exponentially. It really is important to make your best effort to "get it right" for your customer.

> **CIP: Build reliable methodologies that capture customer objections. Know what they resist you doing and why. This must be a holistic view across every facet of your business and will be most useful if both current customers and noncustomers are evaluated.**

As an example: I led a pilot marketing program, and after the we launched our first campaign to acquire new customers, we did research on both responders and nonresponders to understand why some people did not raise their hand. We wanted to know if they had declined to get involved because the value proposition wasn't compelling enough, if they had preferences for a competitive offering, if the communication of the program was not clear, or if there were any other considerations that we had not anticipated.

By actually trying to find out why certain customers had chosen not to respond to us, we gleaned more information about how we were perceived than we would have through simply analyzing the information from people who had responded. It was helpful because it allowed us to repurpose our strategy, and in the end we made double-digit gains in the next phase of the program.

Putting It All into Action

So how can you put a different message or product in the hands of your consumer based on this new and more in-depth view of them? Part of the solution is to actually listen to what you are finding out about your customers, or about the people who choose not to purchase your products.

I have seen major improvements in the companies that I work with when they effectively capture a higher number of attributes in their customer valuation and qualification. Just knowing that someone has a higher visitation or purchase incidence can potentially justify additional marketing spend.

The next step involves designing your product around consumer segments. This need not be an overly complex project. Consider how CPG companies like Procter and Gamble do this today—and very successfully. They manage extensive product portfolios such as detergents: Cheer, Gain, Bold, the Tide Family, Tide Coldwater, Tide TotalCare, Tide to Go, Tide with Febreze, and the list goes on.

The differences in Procter & Gamble's brands are centered on differing customer needs, behaviors, and situations, thus creating the opportunity for distinct product lines.

Another example is women's clothing maker Liz Claiborne and how the portfolio of brands is centered on various customer segments. Each segment has its own brand name and identity. They offer the Dana Buchman brand for professional women; Ellen Tracy for more casual lifestyles; and the Liz Claiborne brand for people with a passion for a more traditional, classic lifestyle.

Chapter 5

So how can you act on this type of information in your business? Consider this examination of how you can take this approach and turn it into a better customer experience:

The customer characteristic or attribute you have observed: Occasion-based buyer—they buy from you only when (XYZ) happens.

Your response for better customer intimacy: Communicate to them and leverage this insight, *when it is relevant* and pertains to this particular circumstance.

EXAMPLE: The hospitality department of a hotel chain has been able to successfully ascertain when you like to travel and whether that travel is surrounded by a particular event, such as the Kentucky Derby. As a result, they are able to offer you special packages and incentives in anticipation of that event. When I worked in package goods, we had an online store that always generated increased volume during certain promotions such as bundled products. Knowing this allowed us to offer upgrades or peripherals during upcoming similar events and helped the customer experience what was relevant to them during times such as Mother's Day or wedding and graduation season. In a business-to-business environment, it translates to knowing your customer's seasonality and high-drive time frames. Know this and reach out with your best, authentic offer at the right time for them.

Other instances will become clear to you in your own inspection. What are the catalysts and barriers for entry? In the retail industry, nearly 40 percent of sales volume occurs in the last two months of the year in some channels. This is one actionable example that we can work with. How? Align a larger portion of the marketing budget to put executions in the market in the months leading up to and within that time frame.

Gathering price strategies, operational strategies, service strategies, and partner strategies to build the ubiquity of the brand during this time of critical decision influence can also serve to make a larger impact in the mind of customers just as they are preparing to spend their money. In financial services, we saw certain life events as a catalyst for financial-product purchase activity. When people move, for example, they are most likely to change or take on a new banking relationship. It was relatively easy to gather data and quantify the opportunity based on knowing the company's current share of that audience and ability to capture additional share of the target. The game-changing action came when resources were decked against this sizeable potential, people, a budget, and autonomy to externalize the brand through partnership programs.

The Home Depot built a similar capability. They know that when people move or buy new houses, they are predisposed to purchasing more product, and usually with a higher frequency right before the event. Every function of the company is aware of and participatory in the "movers initiative," whether it is the sales associate who recognizes the special coupons and offers that these consumers bring into the store, or the credit and billing staffers who send special welcome messages to homeowners.

The Home Depot understands the importance of becoming a partner with home buyers and tenants. They have catered to them by making processes such as updating an online account easier through local support messaging. Solutions are provided to help with the process. They also offer the contact numbers to local utility connections and other task-oriented services. This is low-hanging fruit that can go a long way with the consumer! In my experience in the financial sector, we were able to see a sizeable lift in customer acquisition as a result of initiatives like these.

Avoiding the Land Mines

Before implementing plans like the one used by The Home Depot, you should understand that simply knowing your customers' views and passions isn't enough. You need to have identified characteristics about these customers that motivate you to get involved with them and then build a plan to create commonality.

Chapter 5

QUESTION: What are the desired characteristics that you can identify as motivating you to build inspired relationships with your customers? Based on this insight, do you have an actionable plan? Can you carve out access to this specific audience and treat them more specially and personally as a result? Can you do it with passion, reality, and fun? Can you make a difference that will be transparent for them?

Knowing your customers and then showing them that you know them can be tricky. Sometimes, it is easy to prematurely assume things. It is easy to get it wrong. How many times are you as a consumer on the receiving end of "marketing misfires" every day? How does it make you feel?

People talk about poor or inappropriate assumptions that companies make about them all the time. We all experience it. The good news is that it is wonderful when they get it right! "Wow, thanks, Amazon, this new CD release is something I am interested in buying from you. Thanks for bringing it to my attention. Thanks for knowing me."

The converse of this situation is that it's terribly annoying when organizations get it wrong. Some mistakes are simple to rectify, and I ponder why companies can't do a better job of figuring these out. I can recall hearing customer feedback during my years in the industry, and I always found it compelling to hear their words in research first-hand.

Customers will cry out to organizations to treat them in a way that demonstrates some knowledge of what they want:

"Why do you keep sending me promotions for large women's clothing? I am petite and find it offensive."

"Why do you keep e-mailing me offers to open a new checking account when I already have multiple accounts with you?"

"Why do you keep sending me coupons for your big semi-annual sale when I have never once used a coupon with you? I am not interested."

Chapter 5

"Why do you keep calling me for special hotel rates during weeknights? I have never stayed with you during the week; I am at work and enjoy recreation with you only during weekends."

"Why don't you know me?"

To begin to chip away at this, let's call out some areas where customer-led operation comes to life. Leading customer-focused initiatives you may consider the following:

> QUESTION: *Customer Satisfaction Measurement—What are your scores today? How are they measured? Do you speak only to the existing customer and not potential or competitor ones? What are you doing to take yourself to world class? Are you striving for 80 percent, 90 percent, or more? Where does your competition lie? Have you analyzed and emulated key benchmarks?*

- Marketing, Sales, Service, and Product Improvements: "Broke/Fix resolution"—Identify and address the leading causes of complaints and dissatisfaction. Have you worked with your best customers to identify the "biggies"? How do you determine what matters most to them, versus what is best for you (cost savings)?

- Leverage Insights: Relevant research and knowledge base—Establish fact-based, intelligence-driven functions. How are you capturing customer information today? What other methods and sources can you use to get a better and more recent view of the passions your customers hold dear?

- Customer Information Management: How are you using customer information today? Where are you getting it, and how can sources be expanded? How is it fed into the product, service, experience, sales, promotion, and advertising? What data-sharing capabilities do you have? Do the right decision-makers have access to the customer view so that their executions are more intelligence driven and targeted?

- Culture Development: cultural training, coaching, and reward/incentives and communication of the values that embody an INSPIRED organization

- Marketing and Branding Reinvent: How are you putting your message out there? Can it be better and more personally tailored to your customer and their passion? What ways are you evolving targeting-approach, proposition and offers, articulation, and engagement strategies?

These are a terrific start, and I suggest that as you examine where to place your bets, you keep in mind that a holistic, seamless experience is the goal. ... These efforts must be integrated from a customer perspective.

The slightest disconnect in the food chain of the customer journey can really destroy the natural order of things. It can be corrosive to the equity that you have achieved.

Chapter 6
Step 3: Know What Your Customers Value in a Relationship with You

Now that you've assessed how you view and categorize your customers—and how they view your brand—it's time to begin looking at concrete steps you can take as a small-business owner or brand manager to connect with them.

The first step is to realize that your focus now is value—the value your customers see in what you have to offer—and how you can tailor your offerings to match that perception. You are no longer focusing on a branding strategy that depends on pushy marketing or pricing and discounting to save the day.

Although I recommend examining your pricing and discounting structure, I believe that the long-term implications of relying heavily on discounting are risky. If your company is going to pursue a specific discount position that can be supported over time, be sure that you are aware of how it affects the way your brand is perceived.

In my years of researching and analyzing the customer-company relationship, five common parameters have emerged as themes that apply across multiple industries: Simplicity, Access, Clarity, Quality, and Value. These themes are the nonprice parameters that show a customer that an organization cares about more than just profits.

Chapter 6

As strange as it seems to say that an organization should focus less on profits, the reality is that focusing on these factors will bring greater customer loyalty, a better market position, and inevitably greater stability in tough times. In other words, more profits. Let's take a closer look at each factor.

The Five Factors:

√ **Simplicity**: In the customer's terms, this means, "Make it easy for me to understand what I am getting from you." Customers can't stand to feel as though they've been deceived or confused. Marketing's origins were based around the idea that if you just told customers why your product was better than a competitor's product, they might buy it. How can you be easier to understand for your customer? Businesses now have a powerful tool for direct communication in their Web sites, and customers are flocking to them for information. If you are in a service business, give the customer some examples of what to expect when they do business with you. An auto repair business lists typical wait times for traditional service procedures online and outlines how customers can learn ahead of time what certain services will cost. Help take the mystery out of doing business with you and you'll gain a reputation as a business that makes things easy. If your business is smaller, take the time to ask each customer how you can improve the service experience. Even a few words of advice from a caring customer can show you how to make your transactions simpler. Remember to ask specific questions about the ease of browsing, gathering product information, and purchasing. All three phases are important. Customers don't buy products they don't understand. They want to know what value the product has to them and how that value is in alignment with their personal passions. A customer—and you should know this—likes nothing more than seeing a product that seems to come from people who understand exactly what they need. If you work on cars and have a problem finding the right tool for your application, you'll be *relieved* to pay a little extra when someone, somewhere shows you that they too have experienced the same problem and have come up with a solution. Make sure that you can articulate your product's proposition as a **single clear benefit**.

√ **Access:** "Let me do business in a convenient manner that suits my lifestyle and is seamless." If you've ever tried to purchase a car, you know what access is about. Feeling as though the process by which you purchase a product is opaque and "behind closed doors" is never a good feeling. Customers want to be connected to what matters and want to understand what is influencing their experience. They have questions and want access to honest, straightforward answers. Easy access to people and process is all about time and a respect for what the purchase means to your customer. They appreciate a company that goes out of its way to accommodate their schedule, because anybody facing today's personal and professional demands knows that time is valuable. Always assume that your customer has important demands of their time, even if they don't say as much. Work hard to show them that their time matters as much as yours does. How can you be more accessible to your customer? One opportunity may be to address their ability to get to a solution *faster*. When they have a problem or complaint, give them a way to get to someone who actually knows something about their problem and has the authority to solve it. For example, a small catering business recently set up a dedicated phone number for clients to call if there is an emergency. They realized that sometimes, the people servicing an event can't get away from a job to chase down a problem. This phone number sends an immediate message to the owner that there is a "hot" issue waiting. She can take action or delegate to someone who is free to jump in and help. It allows the customer to feel that the leader is at their disposal. They have a lifeline. Speed to resolution is how access can work for your customer in real time. They will notice the difference and value you for it.

√ **Clarity**: "What is it that you stand for and want me to do with you?" Accept that not every potential consumer is going to want your products. Finding a shared passion means focusing on consumers who share your values and principles. Too many companies exclaim to the world, "We are for everyone." But that means in some ways that they are for no one in particular. General statements don't elicit an emotional connection from the public. A company called Kumon provides after-school and weekend tutoring for grade-school kids. They are not targeting all children, but specifically families who seek extra attention for their children's development and are especially committed to the collaborative effort of improving their academic skills. They make this clear on their Web site where they highlight what their typical (or desired) customer looks like, and that helps make it clear whom they will best be able to service. This kind of upfront communication helps manage expectations. It leads customers to define the desired relationship on their own. This sets up the company for success because the customers are clear in their shared passion for the cause: to unlock the potential in every child.

√ **Quality:** "Give me the best product, brands, and service available to me." Consumers understand better than anyone does what their budgets are. But even limited-budget consumers want value and to feel as though they matter just as much as the consumer who has a lot of money. Work hard to reward your loyal customers, even the ones with limited budgets, and you'll see that long-term relationships can bear fruit as budgets increase. A good example is the generic product market. In the past, generic brands were perceived as the cheap substitute that you used only if you had to. Today, they are not only a respected competitive offering, but in challenging economic times are the *preferred* choice. So how did generic branders achieve that status? Through quality. Commodity product manufacturers are struggling because people have figured out that generic paper towels, peanut butter, and aspirin are just as good as the name brands. If you observe sales trends in many of these categories, you can see it evidenced. People figured out that Kroger or Wal-Mart brand cheese is just as good as Velveeta's cheese. Even Kraft has had to reinvent how it positions itself, because too many high-quality substitutes exist. Give your customers high quality every time and they will move away from other choices and be loyal to you, even when they have less to spend.

√ **Value:** "I want to feel that what I get is worth the investment, and is superior to what I can get from anyone else." Ultimately, consumers want to know that they got their money's worth. It may seem at times that consumers just aren't willing to spend unless products are at a cutthroat rate, especially now when people are afraid of losing their jobs. And you may be right. Some consumers have stopped spending regardless of the values presented to them. But the ones who are spending want to know that your organization has priced your products according to what they are worth, and that you have made an earnest effort to outdo your competition. The goal is to provide increased value while not eroding your bottom line. How can you increase value in ways that matter and not lose money? Consider starting with small, noticeable, even intangible ways. A local wine store near my home has a sign-up list that allows customers to enroll in a monthly invitation to a nice wine-tasting event that they have. Brighton Collectables gives you your purchase in a nice bag wrapped in a ribbon and stuffed with tissue paper. Some auto dealerships call to remind you when your oil change is due. It's these little things that cost virtually nothing that your customers will notice. Then, if you price your products according to their real value, you will demonstrate a genuine commitment to value.

Chapter 6

Below is a chart that looks at where the rubber meets the road. By filling out this chart you'll give yourself a chance to see all sides of a commitment to each of these factors: the tools and techniques your organization can bring to bear; the scope of each project you think will improve customer intimacy; and each project's priority, time commitment, and feasibility.

	Tools and techniques—How can we deliver more of this?	Assignment of scope—My role in improving customer intimacy	Priority and time projection—Feasibility and risk
Simplicity			
Access			
Clarity			
Quality			
Value			

Chapter 6

Below are some of the key initiatives that companies have identified that improve customer-service excellence.

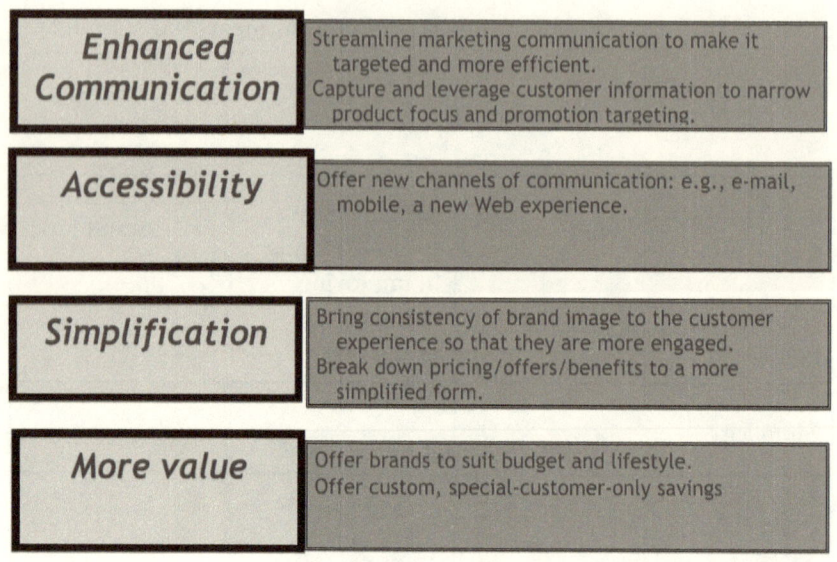

The magnitude of your efforts will depend on your current business circumstances, but I would challenge anyone who says they can't think of a single opportunity within these categories that would capture profitable growth from their valued customers. The important thing is that you write a manifesto and distribute it to the key players in your organization, whether that is ten thousand people or ten people.

Surprisingly, many organizations operate without any form of a written plan for engaging and growing customer relationships. They may have ideas and ambitions but haven't structured those ideas into a plan that aligns with an informed customer view. This makes it really difficult to have a clear idea of where they want to be in three years, or five years.

If companies are willing to spend millions on enterprise architecture, they must know that a clear picture of the physical organization is valuable. So why not have a clear picture of what the people in that organization are working toward with the customer? The manifesto goes beyond any kind of architecture and strikes at the heart of the value question.

The reason I want your manifesto to focus on value is that you want to create a perception that your products are worth the price the consumer must pay for them, even if someone else's offering is slightly cheaper in price.

The customer wants you as an organization to recognize what they value and to see the organization trying its best to provide it. What's more, they want to see that you share the values you've identified in them.

A good example of a clear communication to customers is Ritz-Carlton, which has established itself as a legendary brand in hospitality. The members of the company speak of their credo and corporate philosophy and seem to have a visible commitment to it and a demonstrated passion.

The Ritz credo says, "The Ritz-Carlton is a place where the genuine care and comfort of our guests is our highest mission." The brand managers recognize the power of having that commonality with their customers as illustrated in the company motto: "We are Ladies and Gentlemen serving Ladies and Gentlemen."

Knowing What Your Customers Value Can Help the Misled Brand Manager

In recent years, many brand managers have gone slightly off the tracks. Instead of focusing on rewarding the customer with value, they focused on the short-term desire for driving sales. This is most often achieved through drastic pricing, promotional ads and reaching as many new customers as possible. What about knowing, recognizing, and rewarding existing customers?

As I said in the beginning of this book, the purpose of finding a shared passion with your customers is so that you can move beyond the four Ps of marketing into a space where consumers identify your organization as one that is driven by passionate, focused people who work tirelessly to deliver a satisfying experience. This experience is manifested in each and every place that you interact with your customer and is based on the perception of value.

Most of the touch-points your consumers experience are with people: cashiers, salespeople, technical support people, and others. So if your people don't understand the five factors and don't have a solid manifesto created by their brand managers, what is going to guide them?

In the previous chapter we talked about taking the time to invest in a reliable approach to gaining insight into your customers' desires. You need to have research that clarifies for you what motivates your customer, inspires and interests them, and brings them to the point of willingness to spend so that you know what to instruct your people to do.

Apple has established a legacy for identifying and capitalizing on cutting-edge consumer trends. They keyed in on what would eventually become a movement toward personal expression and individualism. Their computers are not a great deal more advanced than other offerings when it comes to operating systems and functionality. And they recognized that in 1998, when they introduced the iMac.

Because Apple was able to understand that other characteristics of the product could affect passion in their customers, they were able to open some doors of opportunity. Not only did they focus on the "cool" factor, but they created the "I'm a PC" ad campaign to show that their products are inherently more valuable than their competitors'.

They realized that in a world of identical-looking PCs, they could tap into their customers' passion for design and simplicity. They designed a computer that was simple to set up, nice to look at, and totally different from what their competitors were offering. And they promised that it wouldn't crash.

Chapter 6

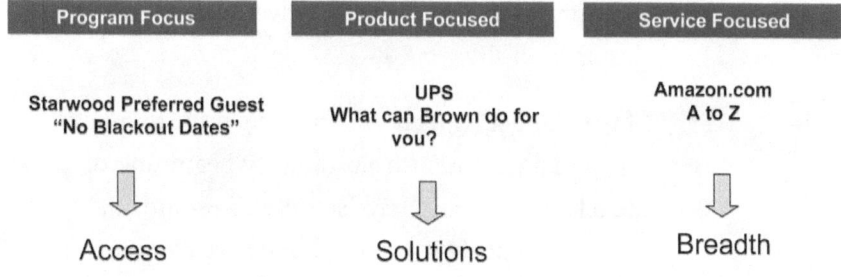

The organizations in this chart have reached out to the buying public and said, "This is how we can meet your needs." They have clear manifestos that say loud and clear what it is they do and how they can help. But these are huge brands. How do you support that kind of communication as a small company, whose logo no one really knows yet?

I think it may be helpful for me to share some of the findings that emerged when I conducted qualitative and quantitative consumer studies on "what they want." What things are always a research favorite with general market testing that I have observed? These findings are the "on the ground" applications of the five factors:

- **Give Me Flexibility:** Create flexible avenues where customers can join in a dialog, select the dialog, or access information—engagement in general. Choice is always key. Customers want to feel an empowered part of the learning, buying, and servicing process. Might they want to learn about you and ask questions online? Or would they prefer to have some way of finding out useful information on your package or through your employees? How many ways can you offer your customer a chance to reach out and plug in? If you're a smaller organization, you'll likely have to depend on each in-person transaction to spread the word. But don't forget to invest in an informative, simple Web site.

- **Make Me Feel Special:** Customers want to qualify for special treatment from the very beginning of the relationship and have status and rewards in recognition of their loyalty. They have chosen you, and they want to be recognized for that. Telling a customer that they will qualify for special benefits only after they have spent a certain amount with your organization is in some ways telling them up front, "We need to get some money out of you before we really care about you as a customer."

- **Give Me Value:** This can be in the form of value-adds—which may be more product, or complimentary benefits or services. They just want to be able to get more. Sometimes, the value-add may be somewhat intangible or subtle. Brand managers are trying to make today's dialog with consumers more relevant to their lifestyles and passions. So, perhaps a more environmentally friendly benefit might be a good value-add. Many customers are receptive to how companies respect the importance of "going green," by offering green-related messages, packages, and processes (recycling, paper usage, and so on). Even as a small organization you are adding meaning to the relationship that you have with your customers by showing them you are offering a product that is thoughtful and useful to them. You are connecting on an emotional level.

- **Give Me Exclusivity:** Customers want access to unique points of interest. Although benefits shouldn't be withheld, there are opportunities for loyal customers to be rewarded, as long as those benefits are explained and offered up front. Then, if the customers continues to spend and remain loyal, you follow up with the promised benefits.

- **Give Me Recognition:** Recognition can be for tenure, a birthday, you name it. Imagine you walk into a restaurant you've frequented and instead of the normal service, the host greets you by name and offers you your usual table. VIP treatment doesn't have to cost a great deal in capital or time. Customers like to be recognized for their business, and that can be as simple as sending a thank-you note to your biggest customers or by going one step further than normal. "You've been great to us and we want to say thank you." That means a lot.

The confused customer: The customer wants what they want. Even if they don't know what that is.

What we've discussed so far is based on the premise that the customer will show you a clear picture of what they value in an organization. But what if the customer is sending mixed signals?

We have been speaking about the importance of research and customer knowledge, but it can be challenging to interpret the truth behind what they say and what they really mean. Sometimes, you can't rely solely on what the customer tells you in his or her own words, because some messages require digging, interpretation, extrapolation, or just plain thought.

Chapter 6

Let me give you an example:

Take the issue of importance or status that a customer achieves with you. How much does it really matter? Do people feel more loyal to you if you let them jump ahead in line because of their status? This notion has often been inconsistently reported, because if you ask a customer how important status is, you'll likely get a lot of denials.

I have seen unanimous denials in customer research when looking into the importance of status, but the reality is a bit different. In the airline and hospitality industry, research has revealed that customers say status is not the most important thing.

Customers say they don't care about being able to jump ahead of people in line or about having a separate line; some indicate that they are embarrassed by the presumption that they are more worthy or important than others. And yet, when we were forced to issue downgrades to customers, look out! The customer-service lines rang off the hook and we were flooded with complaints.

Customers may say that status or rewards are not what they focus on. And in some ways that may be true. But if a reward is promised, the customer will feel entitled to it, assuming they have met their obligations. Offering rewards and tailoring products means not only listening to what the customer says, but also acknowledging human behavior.

I suggest that there is an intangible benefit to recognizing status. Even if customers can't necessarily articulate its importance, be aware that it is an issue. Build in servicing, status-driven experiences as tastefully as possible. Privately, it's okay to make a big deal about a customer, but in public they don't want it acknowledged that they spend a whole heck of a lot with you.

Rewards need to be discreet, because even though feeling special is something most customers enjoy, public spectacle isn't what people buy into when they go to the mall or buy an airline ticket. Why do you think everyone in first class is reading a magazine when everyone else boards the plane? They can't bear the resentment. Openly telling your retail customer, "Congratulations, Mrs. Smith, you have achieved the highest level with us as a super-duper, gold star, elite customer …" in front of her significant other may lead to problems.

In retail, I have seen customers say, "Don't talk about my status when I am making a transaction; I don't want my husband to know how much I spend. … I want that kept just between us." You have to respect that aspect of the consumer's engagement with you.

Other areas of winning value in solidifying your relationship with customers, confused or not, may span the array of rewards certificates, offers, extensions through partnerships with other brands, cause-related tie-ins (donations to their favorite charity), and just plain old cash back. You will have to build out the economics behind the giveback scenarios to determine what makes sense based on the reward structure and redemption forecasts.

In my experience, we've built out fairly robust models to analyze this balance, and it will be important for you to do the same. Put the proper due diligence behind these calculations to match your own circumstances.

Sometimes, a cash-back scenario is simply not worth the expense. Though we are talking about valued relationships, the economic aspect of business can't be ignored. I have seen companies put out programs that they later determine they can't afford and then subsequently discontinue them. This can have a degrading effect on your brand perception and equity, so I suggest you tread cautiously when making this decision.

I Hear You and I'm Listening

When considering improvements to the value your customers see in dealing with you, embrace methods of showing your customers that you know them, you hear them, and you value them. After embarking on a "test" or "pilot program" for a defined period, get some feedback to learn if your efforts are making a difference.

Chapter 6

One example is to send customers information about their interests or industry—it need not be a newsletter or something that requires complex editorial thought. I do business with an agency that sends me articles from time to time, not that were written by them, just industry knowledge, best practices—little nuggets of information that I find useful. E-mail makes this affordable and easy.

Another example might be to give them a "surprise and delight" that they didn't expect. Even if it's just a small gesture, it helps distinguish your company and your brand as one that is willing to show appreciation for the business.

Although we haven't spent a great deal of time talking about the people in your organization, this area of interface is all about the shared passion we've been seeking. What do the people driving your organization care about? What value do they want to project to the world? Do you have a written, emphasized point of focus for your people? If not, then the entire point of this chapter may be lost.

Your customers will see value in your organization only if your employees do first. What are your values and how can you share those with the consumer? Answer that question and the message you send to the consumer will better match the heading over this section.

Chapter 7
Step 4: Become Proactive

If your organization is one that does not have systems in place to generate a true picture of the customer, you cannot become proactive in any meaningful way. Your efforts will be based on a onetime snapshot of your customers—a snapshot that may have been off the mark.

Without a true engagement with your target audience, there can be no understanding of their passions and needs. Without understanding, you are working in the dark, reaching out for any quick opportunity to grab the consumers' attention.

I've found in my experience that many companies do just that. Even large, market-leading companies lose their way when communicating to the customer. Much of it comes back to their inability to generate new and pertinent data about what it is their customers want. But it also comes back to the people in the organization.

The Manifesto

The first step in creating an organization aimed at sharing a passion with the customer is to declare, in specific terms, what your intentions are. If you are a small-business owner, you will soon find that specific, declarative language is helpful in explaining to the customer who you are and how you intend to treat them.

Chapter 7

This process can be encapsulated in a manifesto or "promise" to the customer that serves as a useful reference point for you to revisit and check yourself against at constant intervals. This manifesto will become part of your everyday language; everyone will know it, embrace it, believe in it, and stand behind it.

You may be familiar with how the Disney Company refers to employees as "cast members" who make a promise to create the most memorable, entertaining experience imaginable for their customers. The company's stated mission of quality, creativity, and entertainment is embedded in their promise. Everything involved with the company—its products, its people, and the source of its passion—tells a story.

In fact, Walt Disney consistently lists *optimism* as one of its core values, and the promise of hope that they bring to their customers is key to their success. They believe that entertainment is about hope, aspiration, and positive resolutions. Their promise is consistent and clear to everyone, across the spectrum of properties where customers experience the brand.

When building your own manifesto, create specific statements that make it clear to both customer and employee what is expected. Here's an example:

> We want to help *you*, our best customer, get more from our brand. To this end, we will redesign our engagement to put *you* at the center of the program. Our promise is to provide more personally important attention and to be the best source of quality and value when you seek our services.

A manifesto statement can then be broken down into more specific instructional communications with your employees. If your goal is to have the most knowledgeable staff of any hardware store in your city, then a requirement for continued education can help support your manifesto. The point is to know how each of your promises is going to play out on a cost basis.

Chapter 7

How will *you* structure your plan for delivering on your customer promise? Follow these steps in creating your manifesto and remember that it is a living document that will change as you improve and expand your organization:

- Take the time to think about what it is that you want to promise to your customer. What can you afford to promise them?

- Write your promise down and examine how it fits with your other stated goals in your organization.

- Compare your promise with the things your customers have been telling you over time, and determine how you will show them that you are listening. (This could be done through press releases, advertisements, or an announcement by staff members that they will be offering a new service in-store.)

- Brainstorm ideas in a meeting that includes the major leadership in your organization. When my organization went through this exercise, four or five work streams emerged and we gained clarity about what we wanted to offer our customers.

- When directions are needed or critical paths are chosen, review the manifesto and ask yourself, "Are we living up to the commitment that we have agreed to follow?" It's better to know you're lost than to erroneously believe that you are on track.

Whatever your manifesto becomes, I would suggest focusing on the five key factors from the previous chapter. Any organization that finds itself off-track or losing touch with its customers has to start with itself. Much of what we've focused on in this book so far has been customer-centric. Don't forget, though, that what we started with in Chapter 1 was a discussion of how you as an organizational leader could find commonality with your customers.

Commonality means a mutually shared passion or interest between the consumer and the seller. In this case, you are the seller, but you're also trying to think like a consumer. You know what you want as a consumer, and you know what you like to see when dealing with your bank, your grocery store, or your hotel. Do your people have the same attributes as the ones that please you in a retail exchange? And are the attributes you like the same as those your customers like? Before you can act, make sure you know the answer to these questions.

Now we're going to take a test—a test that will show you whether your perceptions of your customer focus are indeed reality. You can administer this test in your own organization to determine whether or not you are customer-centric. I'll also give you an action plan to follow so that you can bring your data-collection systems up to speed.

Customer-Centric Fitness Test:

- Take a moment to list the top five things that you are focusing on this year. What number of your current efforts will benefit your customer in a new and meaningful way? How will these things change how they see and experience your brand? By 10 percent? Fifty percent? Eighty percent?

- How do you gather and respond to customer insights today? Do you do the "one-off" research projects here and there? Maybe you look at marketing specifically more than the customer view of your brand. Perhaps a situation presented itself to cause you to want to learn more, but the investigation will show only static moments in time. Or do you have ongoing knowledge gathering that is processed and syndicated throughout the organization?

- Do you have a broke/fix effort in place that is looking at the top ten sources of dissatisfaction or causes of customer attrition? Do you know why customers leave you? Is this an ongoing view? Having a method that focuses solely on keeping your organization's passions and actions in line with those of the customer is a fantastic way to watchdog yourself.

- How are you managing customer-satisfaction data? Are all members of your team held accountable? Most organizations measure but fail to follow through with accountability when it might mean making some tough decisions about its people. But without accountability, there are really no true metrics and there's no real change in company culture when something is identified as a problem.

- How well are you leveraging customer information in marketing and product development? Can you describe an example where customer information informed the next big idea that you pursued?

- What customer language do your managers speak, and how does this language get reinforced at all levels? Remember, your people are the ones implementing any decisions made. Do they support what has been set out as companywide practice? Are they

Chapter 7

implementing the new language and new blueprint? Language does matter. It matters a great deal, and if your managers are speaking the right language, it can and should travel down to the people on the front line.

So how did you do? It's okay if you don't feel good about having mastery of all areas; few companies do. Your advancement toward a true customer-centric operation can, and will, occur over time. As I mentioned before, it is a journey. As successful layers are added and customers begin to recognize them, your organization will become that much more effective and efficient.

As your organization becomes more efficient at collecting relevant data and identifying opportunities, you will begin to become a proactive organization, one that actively seeks out opportunities to update or adjust your path through the marketplace.

There is always an opportunity for you to identify a game-changing path, but you just have the knowledge that you need to illuminate that new big idea. You must take the lead in your organization to help establish a tight alignment between your customer and your company's execution. It will absolutely reap immediate and profitable benefits.

An example: Your customer data comes back telling you that in the last month, customers have started to migrate toward less expensive options in several product types. What's more, they are asking for guidance about which product type is both affordable and of good quality. Can you create a venue to address these concerns? Can you change the training of your people or the interface on your Web site to tackle the changing spending habits of your customers? Can you get ahead of your competitors? You can if you pay closer attention to what customers really value than your rivals do.

Chapter 7

The Changing Faces of the Customer

In a study published in *Ad Age* called "The Changing Face of the US Consumer" (July 2008), author Peter Francese points out some interesting trends that I would argue are relevant and can be good sources of action for your business:

> The article says, for example, that the average U.S. head of household average age is now fifty years old. And that more than 80 percent of the growth in the number of households over the next five years will come from those with head-of-household age being fifty-five or older. There was a growth of 23 percent in the number of these households over the previous five years. In the next five years, this group will add more than one million consumers per year to the sixty-five-and-older segment.

What these statistics mean is that you will need to pay careful attention to making sure you give consideration to how these consumers think and behave. The article speaks to the challenge that marketers face in trying to capture the hearts and minds of the risk-averse consumer.

This group of consumers in particular is in charge of families and approaching retirement. That, combined with a lack of confidence in the financial system, will continue to affect the way they spend. And when the head of household—the primary moneymaker—tightens his or her belt, the effect is felt all the way down the line to the teen consumer who once had a lot more discretionary income.

These people are facing a limited-income situation in retirement combined with health care issues and overall retirement asset uncertainty. They are looking for security, stability, and reliability from the purchases they make. So how can you reassure them that your company's execution is in line with their needs?

Chapter 7

The changing ethnic and geographic trends in this country are affecting regional customer interactions. The Northeast is older, with fewer children. The West is younger and more diverse. In California and Texas—two of the largest states—more than half the households are Hispanic, black, multiracial, or Asian.

The immigration impact should be top-of-mind for customer-centric organizations and is a good template for testing the ways in which your organization has chosen to align its execution with the varying wants and needs of its customers. In the past seven years more than 40 percent of U.S. population growth has come from immigration, a situation many organizations have been slow to recognize and embrace.

Companies that embark on diversity marketing and advertising campaigns, community outreach programs, and well-orchestrated PR spins as a result of a lawsuit or some other brand-damaging consequence are a perfect example of this. Companies like Denny's, Texaco, and even Wal-Mart have stepped up their attention to their diverse audience efforts after having experienced damaging, highly publicized litigation losses in recent years.

The Action Plan

Given the information that was just provided by the "Changing Face" insight, what is your plan of attack? Let's apply those facts and take what you know about you and your consumer and advance your approach. It's time to turn your knowledge into an actionable plan that builds your organization into a fleet, proactive body that can capitalize on this trend.

Here are some intuitive and cost-efficient ways to implement a more customer-friendly engagement, based on knowledge like this:

- Think about communication to your customer and how to enhance it for an older audience. Put larger font sizes, for example, in your instructive direct-mail pieces.

- Put more informational narrative in the consumer's hands, available to them in all three channels: Web, call center, and direct mail.

- Community outreach can be a powerful way to connect with your customer's passion. Find ways to be present in the community—I once saw a small business donate bottles of water at a shelter after a hurricane hit the area. There are many low-cost ways to make a difference.

- Consider sponsoring a Web site for a community team (local school or recreational league). Take advertising donations from other local businesses to help share the cost.

- Older consumers are clearly "set in their ways" and will be less receptive to new ideas. How will you choreograph your brand dialog to be more appealing? Realizing that they are looking for guarantees, put your offering to them through an assuring, experienced delivery, and accentuate your proven track record. Offer guarantees and venues for easy and gratifying resolution of problems.

- The value-conscious, older consumer will be looking for a great deal, but with the quality that meets their expectations. Differentiate your product or service or have a "value version" available to them that falls into the appropriate price range. It may be a new derivative of what you currently offer. Do the math and see that the volume of current and potential customers is such a large universe that a price-proper unit tailored for this older consumer will justify the margin concession.

- Give customers a place to have a community and find information that allows them to hear from others like them. The Web is a great place for that—forums, comment sections, chat rooms, and Facebook pages are all ideas that have been widely embraced.

- Provide references and help them connect the dots to be able to figure out all the associated considerations. They are most likely not as technologically savvy as the younger demos that you do business with, so help show them the way.

- Think about the insurance companies that include price comparisons to the competition, or how Dell includes consumer ratings for their computer products so you can see "what others think." Think about their use of icons and symbols to highlight the product features and benefits. In my research projects we have learned that symbols as shorthand help crystallize information in a preferred way. Customers like knowing where they stand, and they like easily recognizable messages that convey that information.

- Find innovative ways to keep the customer "in play" and therefore gain the ability to maintain a constant interest in and consideration for your goods. Customers who are not engaged with your brand on a regular basis will not feel the effect of any new efforts at alignment with their needs. In recent years, General Motors has been offering vehicles under their various brands that have garnered improved ratings from agencies like J.D. Power and Associates. But many consumers were long ago turned off by the lack of quality in GM's cars and were lured into the arms of Toyota, Honda, and other foreign competitors.

- The next set of steps in your action plan involve identifying other consumer trend areas and dissecting them as they pertain to your business. Ideally the steps listed above have taken you down the right path toward actionable items. Now we'll focus on the parts of your organization that you can build right now to support those steps.

Trends in motion:

1. The first step is to institute insight mechanisms that can illuminate trends that are creating a negative impact and to be able to call out the red flags early. What do your customers not like about your company right now and how is that changing? What external factors might be affecting this?

2. Keep the trends front and center so everyone is thinking about them and how to address what is shaping your business. Have the processes in place to make the information impossible to ignore. Too often, the people at the ground level of an organization shield their superiors from bad news. What did we learn from the McDonald's example? That instituting a reporting mechanism that can bypass any interference means that everyone is held to account.

3. Know the trends of your customers that extend beyond your product or industry. Understand how they *live* and how that might shape their decision to do more business with you. Invest in understanding their cultures, lifestyles, and motivations. Know them and capture the ability to be a viable and sustainable part of their lives.

4. Establish systems and processes that recognize new customers versus established ones and that treat them accordingly. Understand the changing complexion of your audience. I suggest that you think through the various life stages of a customer and map out what differentiating strategies can be employed during each one.

The Big Picture

Establishing an action plan that takes into account the broad rainbow of customer interactions, such as the one I've laid out, is a must. The faces of your customers are changing, which means you need to be changing with them.

When you are reactive—even if you are well intentioned—your customer questions the legitimacy of what you offer. They know that it is reactionary and are less likely to accept its authenticity and believability. It will take you that much longer to gain or regain territory as a result, thus costing much more money.

To truly create value and intimacy for your audience you must not manage your interactions with them as isolated, episodic events. Think about them as a sum of actions, or one engagement after another over time. Each one matters, and over time they add up.

Too often, businesses believe that the "next big thing" will keep customers excited and coming back. The ambition is for the new idea: once it's put out in the marketplace, great things will happen and the company will be able to prevent future decline or lag in sales. It's easy to look at the next project with hope that it will reverse fortunes, but it doesn't really explain to you why you hit the decline in the first place.

In these tough economic times, some will say that everyone is experiencing a decline in some form and that drastic times call for drastic measures. But that isn't really a solution that offers a real direction, and it certainly isn't enough to show your customers that you are still passionate about them.

Chapter 7

Putting your hopes into the project that you think will bring in the "big win" for the company – that long-shot hope for a major recovery or rejuvenation . is something we all do as brand managers. How many times have we each chased after the one-off project without really stepping back and keeping the big picture in mind? Think back to when you might have done so and consider what the outcome was. I would bet that even if the project was a success, the underlying structures in the company didn't change and that soon enough you were thinking to yourself, "What can I do that will really put us on the map?"

Let me give you a few examples of what I mean.

EPISODE 1:

When I worked as a marketing vice president in the hospitality and gaming industry, I was often asked to do a study or analysis based on a particular sales situation. When new restaurant venues opened in our hotels, their performance was monitored closely. If they didn't have gangbuster attendance and sales in the first few months, we would be asked to do some research on food preferences, hours of desired dining, price and menu selections, and so on. We were basically told to "Go and figure it out." I remember one new Italian, gourmet restaurant that opened to little fanfare. Unfortunately, there really wasn't the best marketing plan in place for the launch because the restaurant manager thought his brand had enough equity to draw customers in without aggressive advertising. He thought that because his other establishments had done so well in Florida and Chicago, his brand didn't need to be built all over again. His assumption was a stretch to be sure. By assuming that people would instantly recognize his brand and that he would be sought after, he forgot to seek to understand the passions of his new audience. Unfortunately, the customers were not flocking to eat his high-priced meatballs. So, we did some digging to "figure things out."

Chapter 7

BECOMING CUSTOMER-CENTRIC

In the case of the Italian restaurant, a lack of information was impinging on the manager's ability to shape his restaurant to his new audience. In a more customer-driven environment, he not only would have known the desired dining parameters of his customer universe, but would have acted on them and built the environment in a way that was edited for their tastes and needs. We knew the typical demographic statistics, transactions, and customer spend—what we needed to do to take it a step further was carry it into the venues that also constituted the brand experience. Perhaps Italian was not the best choice for that location. If his organization had been intimately familiar with its customers, he would have known the price point and choices that were most important and delivered on that as a natural extension of his promise.

I'm not encouraging you to change your organization in a way that sacrifices your passions or offerings. What I want you to do is be informed about your potential customers and then decide which of them you will target. If an area of potential business is not ready for what you have to offer, reconsider spending the time and money it takes to enter the game.

Let me give you another example:

EPISODE 2:

In my role in the CMO office at Eastman Kodak, I was involved in several initiatives designed to better understand and pursue relationships with multicultural audiences. What a terrific opportunity! The multicultural population in the United States is growing exponentially in size and spending power and has a proven track record of possessing brand-loyal attributes. What I learned was that reacting to a business need in trying to pursue customers, rather than being proactive in wooing them, was limited and unfulfilling. We did our share of what I will call "campaign adoption" where we took communication assets already in existence for the general market and added some in-culture cues to make them fit. But this was not a true customer-centric approach, even though it was a common one. For example, by taking a campaign and adding in actors or models that were multicultural might be viewed as a favorable approach. But if the depictions were not authentic or true to how those cultures lived their lives, they would pick up on it and feel that it was "not for them". When a message is designed specifically for an audience, the representation is true: end-to-end. The music, the setting, the hairstyles, the vehicles, the situation, the verbal references and even the humor are all appropriately designed in a way that the audience can relate to. They know that this company is for and about their needs. There is so much to consider – and remember, it is all intuitive for your customer.

Companies often look to save marketing investment by adapting existing products to address a new market need. But are they really doing themselves any favors? As mentioned in previous chapters, today's consumers are savvy. They understand when they are being treated as an afterthought, and they act accordingly. If an organization really values the business of a particular customer segment, then it ought to convey that to the customer, which is ultimately the lesson we learned.

BECOMING CUSTOMER-CENTRIC

In an act of forward thinking, these organizations evolved to more specifically define the target audience and to qualify the best customers through robust valuation methods. Then, based on this knowledge, we created custom campaigns designed to target the specific geographies and demographics we were trying to reach. It was not just the general market brochure or advertising simply translated into Spanish and placed across the spectrum of media we were using. It became a laser-focused view of the priority jurisdictions and locals, and added (through research and analysis) the relevant proposition—one that would naturally and authentically resonate. At Bank of America, we saw new bank account acquisition skyrocket in the target communities and found other key performance measures to keep track of successful execution. We were thinking about the long-term, big picture from a customer point of view, and not just jumping on the problem or need of the moment. This shift in thinking transformed our results and helped build new sources of value for the brand.

If you're a small-business owner and don't have access to in-depth marketing such as this, then consider your manifesto. Whom are you trying to reach? If your customers are international or online, as is the case with some smaller eBay businesses, can you hire a translator to improve communications on your site? Can you extend your hours of operations to allow for these international customers to contact customer service?

If you can't afford measures like these, consider smaller tokens that will still demonstrate your passion for the customer's values. Do you have an FAQ that is written from the perspective of a real customer? Are you doing enough to learn about the markets where your products are going? If you are, then you might be able to identify new opportunities.

1.

2.

3.

4.

Chapter 8
Step 5: Attack the Causes of Mediocrity

By now I hope you have some idea of where everyone stands in the customer-company relationship. You should know what your customers think of you and what you hope for from them.

I hope you've also found some shared passion you think will help to bridge any gaps that may exist between you and the desired business outcomes you're striving to achieve. This is often not an easy process, and I expect you will still have some questions about the nuts and bolts of this transformation you've undertaken. After all, shifting an organization of any size from one that is distracted by short-term demands to one that is visionary and guided by a leading passion and principle is not easy.

There are pitfalls you need to be aware of as you begin the real actionable items I've laid out for you in the previous steps. It's not uncommon for organizations to get lost in the middle of their transformation. I hope, though, that what you've done so far has served to get you closer to embracing the concept of moving toward gaining share through customer intimacy.

The point of distinction you're trying to realize for your brand is to deliver "above and beyond" intimacy. It's not just what the customer might expect, but what they would never have expected. This form of intimacy will drive the business ambitions that you have:

Chapter 8

- Increase customer share for your business.

    - Ultimately you want the customers in your area of operations to look to you as the leader of the pack.

- Increase the stamina and strength of your relationships.

    Attracting new customers is not enough. Too often today's brand marketers are comfortable with the churn that's been created by the overload of advertisements customers see and by the speed with which they can change allegiances. Pursuing long-term customer relationships is still worth the effort.

- Increase your value to the customer with compelling offerings.

    - What this work will come down to ultimately is the product or service you offer to the customer. It's one thing for a customer to tell a friend they were treated well. But if that compliment is accompanied by a pause and then the phrase, "But the food wasn't any good," or "You know so-and-so makes a better DVD player," then the compliment is invalid

- Get a greater return from your customer relationship efforts.

    - What you want is a customer who is glad to spend their money with you, a customer that holds your organization in high regard and will spend their money on the items you provide regardless of the economy. You want to be held in the same regard as Campbell's Soup and Johnson & Johnson.

Chapter 8

You may already be doing a decent job of tackling these ambitions today. But, it is not enough to just "satisfy" a customer in today's economy. Customers are just a mouse click away from experiencing, and potentially buying from, your competitors. Are you going to be ready when the next customer logs on to your Web site, or goes to your stores and talks with your associates? How will you convince your people that the passionate ground you want to share with your customer is worth supporting?

Your first goal in Step 5 is to avoid these common pitfalls. It may seem odd to focus on accomplishing your goals by *not* doing something, but success in this endeavor is as much about avoiding mistakes as it is about embracing new ideas. You're endeavoring to make real changes in your organization, and you need to make sure those changes don't upset your customers. People sometimes react badly to change, even if the intended outcome is a good one.

1. Do Not Become "That" Company.

> Labels are a dangerous thing. Once you're labeled in the public arena, you're most likely going to be associated with whatever attributes the label carries with it … and for a long time. In 2007, Sprint received notable coverage and a reputation for their poor customer service. They ranked at the top of MSN Money's survey called the Hall of Shame, which ranked the worst companies for customer service. Sprint spokespeople acknowledged that the company had room for improvement, but when it came to the poll, Sprint was the clear loser. The company was given a "poor" rating by 40 percent of those poll respondents who had an opinion about the company. No other company had more than 30 percent by that measure. Sprint's customer service was considered "fair" by 28 percent of respondents who rated its service, "good" by 25 percent, and "excellent" by just 7 percent. Roni Singleton, a Sprint spokeswoman, said, "There are definitely areas within customer

service where we need to improve. Our CEO and others all have said we're committed to that."

But was it enough to convince the public that they really were committed? A year later, in 2008 they improved and were ranked third, but their reputation is still in turmoil—at the end of 2008, their stock was trading at $1.70. They made some improvements to that price in early 2009, moving their stock to just over $5 in early June, but that's a value of less than one-fifth of what the stock was trading for in early 2005.

You must make it clear to your customers that any changes made are for their benefit, and that you are above all else committed to their satisfaction. Otherwise, you'll be where Sprint is, fighting and clawing your way back.

2. Be Willing to Face Adversity Head-On.

Any journey toward a new source of value will involve facing points of pain, to be sure. The economics, the risk, the initial failures, lack of universal consensus, lack of the proper resources, and just plain lack of faith can all play into the outcome. As I've said before, change is sometimes unwelcome by those who have to do the changing. Telling an employee that their interactions with customers leave room for improvement can be seen as an insult. There may be a loss of loyalty from some employees or a backlash from managers who are told to change their styles. But it has to be done.

When I think of facing adversity, I think of my experience with Kodak and all the difficult conversations that took place as the company struggled to make the transition to a digital platform. As we closely followed consumer trends, early adopters were signaling the trend to come: technology was ubiquitous, margin was tight, and the cash cow of the company, film, was in decline. In the time that it took the large multinational company to face the reality and set a portfolio reinvention in motion, a lot had changed and financial pain was endured throughout the organization.

But their story is a good one. Because of the strong conviction of the leaders of the company and their belief in the power of the brand and what it had to offer, new ideas turned into some highly competitive and exciting product lines that have kept them at the top of the market in their industry.

3. Get Out of Your Own Way.

> I have seen it time and again: the organizational silos, territorialism, accountability gaps, conflicting objectives, talent and knowledge gaps, and even leadership conflicts. They occur in every organization and they are the result of a poor top-down design. Every group is left to its own devices, and they operate without a clear sense of purpose. The results are predictable: when it comes time to change, you hear nothing but bickering as everyone jockeys for credit or for an excuse for what went wrong.
>
> Organizations plagued with these attributes are destined for failed plans and the absence of real change. A good way to avoid these problems is to guide the company with a clear and sustainable vision; a purposeful and passionate stance that everyone can get behind. Not everyone will, and if the dissention is strong enough, and the "rebellion" long enough, it begs the question, who's really in charge? Do you have problems that are larger than just a weak manifesto?

Chapter 8

Chipotle is a shining example of an organization that was founded on a relatively simple principle, and their results are hard to argue with. The restaurant chain has been a strong performer even during the tough economic climate.

During the nine months ending on September 30, 2008, Chipotle increased revenues 23.8 percent to $986 million. That's in comparison to comparable restaurant chains that saw just 6.6 percent growth. Chipotle had a restaurant-level operating margin of 21.7 percent. And it all started with company founder Steve Ells's simple aims: to create the hottest fast-food company in the country and to serve all-natural ingredients to an audience looking for something different from the regular burger chains.

Ells is quoted on the Chipotle Web site as saying the following:

What I wanted to do was simple: apply the techniques I had learned at the Culinary Institute of America and in professional kitchens into making great tasting burritos and tacos with the best ingredients I could find. Price them reasonably and serve them up in a hip, friendly, casual environment. The concept seemed to me straightforward and altogether needed. Done well, it would let me show that food that was made fast didn't have to be like typical fast-food.

Ells has gone one step further with his chain. He's attached his passion for good food and fun dining to a cause that's near to his heart: the humane treatment of animals. In 2001, Chipotle began buying their pork only from family farms that treated their animals humanely and that raised them without antibiotics. It was a step that not only satisfied a passion of the company founder, but also was in line with the thinking of millions of Americans (potential customers) who wanted to see improvements to the way farms were run.

> "We began buying our pork from family farms like Paul's that raise pigs humanely and without antibiotics," Ells is quoted as saying. His move to better farming suppliers was made out of passion and concern. And naturally, customers who share that passion follow suit.
>
> Ells was also smart enough to know that his passionate approach to food was not a sure thing, and that he always had to keep his customers in mind.
>
> Food with integrity is our mission, but we know that at the end of the day, we can't judge our own integrity. That's for our customers to decide. So all I can say is that we are still leading from what we believe is right, and constantly striving to improve the way we do things.

4. Don't Keep Too Many Cooks in the Kitchen.

> What Steve Ells has been able to do is keep his personal vision for his chain at the forefront of its operations. He has kept his leadership on a track that he decided long ago, and that's a powerful ability.
>
> Many companies are beholden to multiheaded monsters: they have to please the shareholders, the board of directors, their management, and their customers. That's a tall order. But is there really any alternative to having a clear direction set by the leadership of a clearly defined hierarchy? I would suggest that there is: confusion and a waste of resources and time that leads to diminished sales.

5. Make Partnerships Work with Your Passions.

> There's nothing worse than creating an allegiance that ends up hijacking your vision for your company. It happens all too often as conflicting passions and interests tear apart the best intentions of companies that set out to connect with their customers.
>
> It's wonderful to have alliances, agencies, and consultants helping you get to where you want to be, but the journey is still a process that you must own. Ownership has to be clearly in the hands of the people whose vision is being implemented; otherwise there is no compass.
>
> An example of a successful partnership:
>
> Saxonia is a German company that specializes in engineering, special press equipment, and tooling. They needed a partner in the North American market, so they joined forces with Stampings Incorporated based in Fraser, Michigan.
>
> Saxonia provides the expertise and physical product, and Stampings handles the sales, marketing, and customer service support in the United States. What was key to the agreement was that it was detailed and made clear who was responsible for what.
>
> Stampings has also been able to develop further successful partnerships with customers because they understand that every detail needs to be addressed ahead of time, using cross-functional teams that are enabled to make decisions.

6. Making It All Make Cents

> All too often, I've seen the tendency by organizations to overinvest in technology, customer management systems, and human capital incentives based on a return or break-even curve that is much too steep. Then the internal interest level subsides, second-guessing occurs, and all of a sudden you have the famous disappearing act where the idea somehow gets lost in the organization.
>
> Employees inevitably think the program has failed to live up to the promises of its champions. The real challenge lies in your ability to engineer the economics properly and allow for sufficient scope and scale for ramp-up to the point when critical mass is achieved. To accelerate the return that you can get from your customer management and loyalty initiatives, do everything possible to hold the customer accountable. Don't hesitate to ask more of them—after all, relationships are built on reciprocity! You can achieve this through some of the following steps:
>
> - Encourage them—through education, incentives, and selective product matching—to buy more from you, across the product line, and more frequently.
>
> - Encourage them to buy from you through multiple channels and venues. We have seen that multichannel customers are more profitable and susceptible to cross-brand marketing and promotion.
>
> - Ask them for information to help you sell to them more profitably.
>
> - Don't reward all customers, just the best and most profitable.

Chapter 8

- Create vehicles for lower-cost, self-service functionality that require less human intervention from your employees.

As you consider the programs that you want to put in place to help you manage and drive relationships, think creatively about ways to garner incremental revenue streams. American Airlines established a loyalty program on a points-based currency like many relationship-marketing programs do today.

What is interesting about the American Airlines model is the fact that whereas many loyalty programs are guilty of unpredictable expense appreciation, much to the aggravation of their managers, American's program operates as its own profit center. The AAdvantage program sells points to other businesses, who use them to reward their clients and customers. Companies such as Citigroup, hospitality companies, and other Fortune 500 companies like Kellogg's buy the points for distribution as a value-add for their associates.

In the article "Your Loyalty Program Is Betraying You" (HBR press,) authors Nunes and Dreze correctly point out the following:

Companies of all kinds are killing off their loyalty initiatives. Why? Most programs don't produce the results they promise: lower customer churn, higher sales and profitability, and more valuable insights into customer behavior.

The authors suggest that no program can ensure unprecedented devotion to your company and they're right. Yet, properly designed and implemented, rewards programs will yield longer relationships with happier customers—thus ensuring you the best kind of competitive advantage. The authors also cite companies with models that failed and were eventually discontinued as lessons learned about what not to do. Even successful, forward-thinking companies put together programs that didn't make it, like Subway and eBay. But when done right, companies reap the benefits.

Each of these pitfalls is something you need to pay attention to as someone pushing for positive change in your organization. Don't become overly cautious, though. Companies that understand calculated risks are more nimble than companies that are paralyzed by fear of failure. Up next, we'll start dealing with the details of creating a passionate workforce beyond the manifesto.

Chapter 9
Step 6: Ignite the Power of People—Building and Nurturing the Winning Culture

In the previous chapter we talked about the many pitfalls that can occur when managing change toward customer-centricity. It's not an easy task, and if you reread some of the pitfalls, including "Get Out of Your Own Way" and "Don't Keep Too Many Cooks in the Kitchen," you'll realize that many of them will involve your own people.

What is reality, though, is that the employees who implement any plans that you've made must be on board. They absolutely must believe that the changes they are being tasked with are going to benefit the company and themselves.

Getting your people to believe this is made easier, of course, if they share some of the passion that the organization's leadership has for a concept or product. They'll gladly get behind what you propose because they believe as you do.

For the most part, though, it is highly likely that you will have people who come from both camps: the believers who are ready to get on board and the pessimists who will resist any form of change until they see what's in it for them.

Chapter 9

I have seen it occur in every organization that I have worked in, big and small. The advantage comes when this reality is faced head on—when the leaders recognize that they have some employees who are willing and enthusiastic about the new customer mind-set and another group that understands, but still needs real encouragement to get there. Either way, it is important to note that it will take energy and extraordinary leadership to get everyone operating at peak efficiency.

The Leadership

I have worked for and studied some of the largest and most successful companies in the world. Certain patterns show up time and again. Not only do these companies follow the steps I've outlined so far, but they have something beyond the nuts and bolts, beyond the desire to change. They have the leadership and the fortitude to push through the pitfalls I've outlined in order to actually make something great happen.

What are the leadership traits that successful companies possess to get it done?

- Ability to demonstrate unwavering purpose and conviction
    - If the people in your organization have seen leadership commit, and then abandon, past plans, they will likely not jump on board for any new plans. There must be a demonstrated sense that any new initiatives are supported by everyone at the top, and that there is a real intention to follow through on ideas that are intended to improve the relationship with the customers.

- Set the standard on a fact basis, with an exacting attention to detail.

- Initiatives that enjoy well-researched motivations are sure to garner greater support from your people. Nobody likes to waste time and effort on something that is supported by only a hunch. Although passion is the centerpiece of what we're trying to achieve, there must of course be a business justification to go along with it.

- Act with urgency and determination to succeed.
  - It's easy to get people behind an idea in the beginning stages; none of the work has started yet and there's been no cost to pay. But how long do you think support for your ideas will last should you get bogged down in the planning stages or should other people detect any semblance of doubt from you? I would say not long.

- Visibly telegraph the ambition and business growth potential to inspire teams.
  - Tell them why this is great, both for them and for the customer! With a clear picture of where they are to go, your teams will feel a greater sense of direction and purpose. No one wants to set out on a journey that will require some painful choices unless they are fairly certain of the payoff. Your employees are people, and sometimes people need to know what's in it for them before they're willing to walk the plank for you.

- Foster the interactions that bring the right people to the table.
  - The fact is that during a time of great change, there will be a division in some camps. You want

people at the table who understand the urgency of what you're trying to accomplish. In this economy there is little time to fight the idea of change. Change is a requirement for many, not a choice. The question is, are you going to make the right changes?

- Keep the faith in the face of obstacles.
  - Any brand marketer who has seen enough campaigns will tell you that setbacks are a certainty, not a possibility. Things change, and sometimes for the worse. Keeping the faith is made easier when people in the organization have a leader who shows clarity of purpose and an unwavering belief that they are capable of achieving the best possible outcomes with their customers.

To gain the necessary cultural energy and spirit to manage the shift to a customer-centric culture, you will want to foster an environment of creativity, imagination, and a desire for speed-to-market. I would suggest that you do as much as possible to avoid letting bureaucracy and hierarchy get in the way.

Through discipline, your teams can move the business forward while maintaining adherence to your framework design and customer manifesto (promise). Jim Collins, the author of *Good to Great,* suggests that to manage a great company, leaders must build a culture around the idea of freedom and responsibility. They must fill the culture with people who are self-disciplined. They should create a "Stop Doing" list and unplug the extraneous actions that contribute nothing to the purpose of the organization.

In the age of virtual communication and management, it is much more feasible to "stop doing" some of the destructive practices that bog down many an organization, such as holding too many meetings, requiring too many presentations and too many approvals, changing directions too often, and unnecessary redundancy.

One way to help eliminate these tendencies is through a communication architecture that is part of your framework. Have your self-disciplined leaders manage the work stream through this framework and you'll experience a drastic reduction in the redundant communications so many companies seem to live by.

Allow me to highlight an example of what I mean:

The department store Nordstrom was facing the challenge of becoming a brand that is of and for a "mature" customer. Even with their fresh, innovative designs and invigorating, stylish store environment, the typical customer they attracted skewed toward an older demographic. They recognized the importance of bringing a customer focus to their culture and brought their methods to life in a highly successful way.

Leaders began to educate themselves on the characteristics of the millennial customer (typically categorized as someone born between 1982 and 2002). They helped bring the company culture up to speed on the importance of these customers and charged them with the responsibility for building new concepts that targeted and won over this younger audience.

Through desire and accountability, Nordstrom built some interesting lifestyle strategies that were supported by major marketing efforts and campaigns. These programs came to life through the desire and passion of both the marketers and the employees. What was once a somewhat "stuffy" department store was quickly transformed into an engaging source for youth through some of the following outlets:

- Twitter posts on upcoming fashion events, supported by product the younger customer wants

- Facebook pages on "fashion status" that allow the customer to post his or her style and mood and track those of their friends

- Discussion boards on the hot topics of the day
- Blogging from the floor about events, trends, menswear, and the latest designer news for those who want to be in the know

Responses have been strong and consistent, and the company has seen the benefits in their sales performance. It's a terrific example of a company that overcame public perceptions through an active, well-structured plan that was supported by the company's people. The cultural mind-set that embraced a customer opportunity transformed a company into one with a whole new captive audience ready to build new relationships with a brand.

The Customer Experience

The ability and attitude of your people can significantly impact how customer experiences unfold. Researchers at J.D. Power and Associates found in a study published in June 2008 in *The Wall Street Journal* that customer satisfaction with the North American airline industry had hit a three-year low. The research firm said customers are less concerned about paying higher fees than about what they see as a decline in the quality of customer service.

The survey, which questioned more than nineteen thousand business and leisure travelers, found that customers generally understand that with the skyrocketing price of jet fuel in recent years, airlines need to charge more for tickets and add fees for services that used to be free. But, airline passengers also said there has been a marked decline in the way airline employees treat customers.

From workers at ticket counters to the onboard crew, employees are less helpful and knowledgeable than they were in 2007, the survey found. The decline in customer service has come from staff cutbacks at airlines, as well as tougher working conditions for employees, who took cuts in pay and benefits during the airline downturn early in the decade.

Unfortunately, these changes translated into poor attitudes and service. I have experienced this personally and would guess that you have as well. This survey further illustrates the need for airlines to invest in their employees as a means to enhance the customer experience, as there is a strong connection between employee satisfaction and customer satisfaction.

Keeping It Simple

One of the things I've found that best helps employees get on board with a new idea is keeping the scope of a project realistic. Employees are not fools, and they have limits to what they will commit to if it seems a project has a scattered focus.

Your people will be better able to remain inspired and properly focused if they believe that changes are both realistic and practical. That doesn't mean you have to abandon your grand dreams for your organization, but you had better have a distinct set of smaller steps in place to build toward those dreams. Learn from the airline industry and realize that cost-cutting measures as they relate to employees will almost always have a negative impact on the customer experience if not handled properly.

Every organization has been faced with tough choices in this economy. It's not unusual for companies to have to cut dozens or even thousands of jobs. If this is the case with your organization, then realize that changes you hope to make are going to be made in the shadow of some discontent from your workers.

Don't try to tackle too many opportunities at once. Scope creep that eventually led to self-destruction has killed more organizational ambitions than not pursuing enough opportunities in the first place.

Chapter 9

Maintain the stamina to endure the long haul. Involve helpful ambassadors who are "believers" who may be able to fly below the radar and help move the cause forward. These people can help lift the spirits of those around them and act as motivation for employees who may not share the great enthusiasm of these ambassadors.

Get alignment as much as you can around the language of a customer-first movement. What are the objectives, who will be a participant in making it happen, how will this help the company win? How will you syndicate your progress and risks?

Getting everyone on the same page in advance is helpful, but not always a failsafe. At times, a course correction will be needed. I have personally experienced this "cold feet" syndrome, and it can feel like a surprise attack. It can feel like things have been thrown off the tracks. But not to worry: it happens and is normal.

People are people, and that means they change their minds and may question if something new can really work. It's okay. Stay the course, build in test-and-learn capabilities to grow confidence in the viability of it all, and remember, you are all working to create a bigger picture.

Below is a framework that may be useful in illustrating how the three key components of your company's operation work together to contribute to the overall strength and growth of your organization. I think of your passion and capabilities at the core of what you do best as the *foundation*. The pillars that serve to support and grow your infrastructure are fueled by these foundational elements.

As you get better and more adept at navigating the components in ways that serve as the best of a customer-centric organization, achievements such as earning a reputation for product excellence and service superiority will surely come along. And that's a winning combination!

Keep in mind that even if your organization is a small one, you can rely on these pillars as you scale your operations up. Staying ahead of the competition, maintaining service excellence, and staying loyal to your core customer's desire are all actions that apply to business in every category.

A person with a passion that is not acted on is merely a dreamer.

Chapter 9

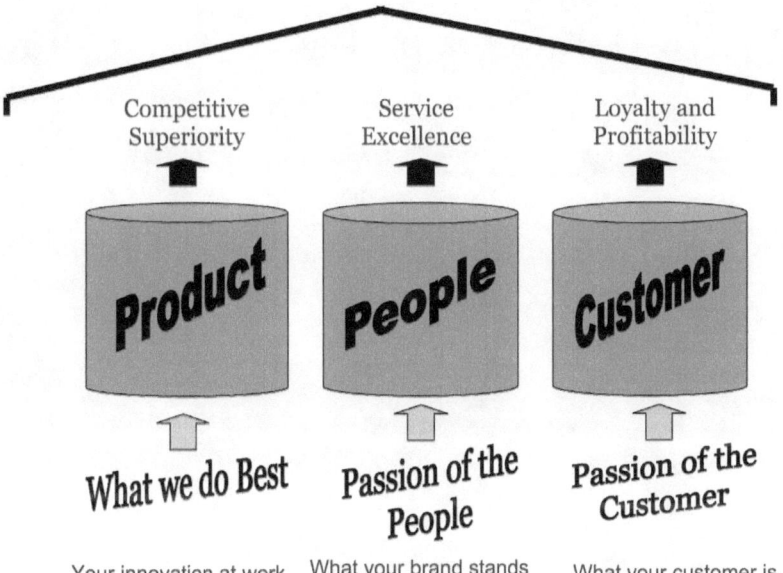

CUSTOMER INSPIRED MARKETING 121

Chapter 10
Step 7: The Small-Business Owner: Overcoming the Challenges of Limited Resources

The steps outlined so far involve a great deal of work and time to execute correctly. You are tackling not only a down economy but also the attitudes and habits of your own employees, your personal fears, and the chance that the changes you make will not work.

If you're a small-business owner, you may be worried that you don't have the resources to tackle the steps outlined in this book. After all, how are you going to gather marketing data and survey your customers when you're the only one working in the business?

You've already taken the first step if you've read this book. You've realized that marketing for the quick sale, depending on discounting or even fear-driven marketing and chasing the "home-run" product are all paths to eventual failure. You realize that you want to connect with your customer and form a long-term relationship based on shared values and equal exchanges.

How you go about implementing these steps will depend greatly on your budget, your goals, and your ability to conceptualize the customer. With little money and limited resources, a small-business owner has to depend more on voluntary customer feedback in one-to-one situations or on a Web site. There is the tendency to overreact to one customer's desires because you don't know if others feel the same way.

As you build your business, it is important to understand that right now you may not be able to carry out some of the steps in this book on a large scale. What you can do is adapt them to your needs.

Have an Inspired and Informed View of Your Customer:

This one is easier for the small-business owner than for the large corporation. You have fewer customers and the chance to interact one-on-one through e-mails, phone calls, or even walk-ins. This step is doable and should be the first for the small-business owner after examining your own passions.

1. Determine How Your Customer Views You:

This may be harder, but it is not impossible. If you include with your product delivery the instructions to fill out a survey online (even a simple one), you may find that customers are willing to cooperate. eBay has jumped onto this need of small-business owners by including feedback for its auctioneers. You can do the same in a simple Web site and offer future discounts to those people who fill out a survey for you.

2. Know What Your Customers *Value* in a Relationship With You:

As a smaller-business owner, you will be faced with the realization that staying true to your vision and your core beliefs will at times have to substitute for in-depth, advanced marketing and large ad spends. As Chipotle showed us, following a passion can be risky. In this step you will need to rely on both your records of sales in the past and your understanding of your market as it stands now. If you don't have detailed records of your sales, then begin immediately keeping them. Having a track record of what has sold well will help to guide your understanding of what your customers value. Also, compare yourself with your competitors. What do you have that they do not? What do they have that you do not? And where do you stand in the marketplace relative to them? These questions will help you understand why people are drawn to your business and what attributes you might adopt based on the success of your competitors.

3. Becoming Proactive:

Becoming proactive is not something that depends heavily on a long track record of in-depth marketing analysis. These tools surely help in determining how a market is trending, but not having them won't keep you from determining where you want to ultimately be. If your manifesto is strong and you have a good sense of where you stand in the marketplace, you can move forward on your plans and aspirations. Several tools will help you understand the marketplace, even on a budget:

Competitor reactions to your offerings. If they react quickly and forcefully, you know that your offerings are a threat and are therefore likely making an impression with customers.

Product transitions among your customers. If you find that customers are transitioning to a new version of a product or service, you can stay ahead of the curve.

Notes and observations from your own experiences. What in the marketplace has you excited? What would you like to see offered to you? You're passionate about what you do, and that means you care deeply about learning the ins and outs of the business. That will keep you ahead of complacent competitors.

Attacking the Causes of Mediocrity:

The pitfalls in this step apply to everyone. If you're a small organization and have to partner with someone, you now know what to look out for. You are capable of working out details ahead of signing contracts, and you are already in the habit of leading the way with your employees. Just make sure you keep it that way as you scale up in size. Remember to keep your mission statements in writing for all to see.

Chapter 10

Ignite the Power of People—Building and Nurturing the Winning Culture:

As a small-business owner, you have the advantage of fewer employees and divisions to restructure. With an older, larger company the sales pitch from leadership is much, much harder. They have to somehow convince each division that changes are both profitable and desirable. In a smaller organization, communicating that message can be done in person to each employee. Instead of an interoffice memo, you can rely on brainstorming sessions, casual pep rallies, and the knowledge that your leadership is visible to all.

Being a small-business owner can be daunting. You have major questions to deal with—insurance and benefits, energy costs, a shrinking market—and although some of these are outside the scope of this book, the ideas inherent to customer-inspired marketing are universal.

Your customers want to feel valued. They want to know that you are treating them as special, that your products are priced fairly, and that all communications with them will be transparent and straightforward.

Above all, though, remember that your passions are what got you into your business in the first place. What are they telling you? Have you lost your way? Are you doing the things you'd want to see in a business you purchase from? If not, go back to the beginning of this book and start to apply these principles to your operations, no matter the size.

Chapter 11
Step 8: Celebrate and Build for the Future

Now that you understand with complete confidence where, in your pursuit of customer relationships, the sweet spot exists for both your company and your customer, you are on your way to creating a passionate brand. So celebrate!

Although your work is certainly not done, you've made huge leaps by now in understanding what it is that makes companies into "names" rather than brands. I don't expect you to build a Johnson & Johnson or Apple through just reading this book, but I do want you to garner the same loyalty from your customers.

And you can do that with a return to honest marketing, a product and service offering that embraces your core values, and a deeper understanding of who your desired customer is now and is going to be in the future.

Realize that by openly confronting your own notions about your customers, organization, and personal passions, you have gone further than most companies are ever willing to go. Honesty is sometimes painful, especially when it reveals that your brand is none too popular. But at least now you know who you are.

Chapter 11

To begin this final chapter, we're going to recap some of the lessons learned earlier in the book. Then we'll talk about the ways you can ensure that meaningful changes are also long-lasting changes.

The characteristics of a passionate brand:

- A passionate brand knows what it stands for and has the courage to do so in a way that is distinctly different from the competition.

- A passionate brand is maintained by people who lead from the heart.

- A passionate brand seeks to become the ultimate representation of its authentic self.

- A passionate brand has the energy and drive to always be fresh and inspiring in new ways while maintaining consistent core themes.

- A passionate brand is deeply connected to its community. It has an image, a representation, and a depth of pride and commitment that can't be missed. Hershey is a product of Hershey, Pennsylvania, Wal-Mart of Bentonville, Arkansas, and so on.

- A passionate brand is true to its core values and its founding principles. Remember that the customer appreciates the "specialness" that is your brand and that bigger is not always better. Ubiquity puts you in a different place in their hearts. Wolfgang Puck is now in airports, Starbucks is now in grocery stores, and Krispy Kreme doughnuts are now at local gas stations. Before you expand yourself into commonality and venture into new exposure, remember what your passion is and think about whether your mission will still be fulfilled when your brand is known for its ubiquity and not its uniqueness.

These characteristics are vitally important to any organization that plans on *showing* their customers who the company is. And although it's wonderful that you've started this process and ideally have committed to forming a more passionate company, questions still remain.

Making It Last

To maintain that standing in the hearts and minds of your customers, it is important to realize the transient nature of things. The world around you and your customers will inevitably change, so how do you sustain an inspired and passionate relationship over time? You start by having the right core values, as we have discussed—and by building in some methods for sustaining them. I offer the following checklist to get started:

1. Ask yourself these questions: Is what you stand for—your values, your promise, your passion—something that will be your passion tomorrow? What about a year from now? Will your key strategy become stale or obsolete over time?

Remember in your search for a passionate base not to drill down to a tiny, specific feature that will have no sustainability. If a brand in the automotive industry had chosen to hang its hat on remote-control keyless entry back when that technology was new and interesting, it would have been in trouble in short order. You can see that it clearly wouldn't hold up as a very important difference today, because everyone has it. Plus, in today's times, people essentially have a personal computer system as part of their vehicles: iPod, music and media management, cell phone interface, navigation, home service access—you name it. The game is much bigger than it was five years ago. So is the manifestation of your passion sustainable?

2. Will your product or service distinction matter to your customer over time?

When you consider some obvious categories like technology and innovation, you can think about how important that will be for your customer in the future. Federal Express leads with innovation in its supply chain, information technology, and tracking systems, for example. The brand's ability to maintain a position as the "absolutely, positively" brand is well supported by the innovative technology that helps service its customers. This example is a good one because in the shipping industry, customers care about the things that FedEx is focusing on: speed, reliability, and ease of interaction.

3. Find ways to spark creativity and imagination into your offering so that you can take a leap above and beyond your traditional path.

Your data tells you one thing, but what creativity can you layer on to the facts to ignite something really exciting? Southwest Airlines was creative in how they defined their point of difference through the elimination of basic services—no reserved seats, for example. This helped them take out cost and serve the customer more economically. While focusing on a perceived negative—the removal of services—Southwest was able to spin the changes as making the airline more egalitarian.

The Levi's brand has known its passion for more than a hundred years, and what core values matter most. They have always been a pioneer in apparel, but they are also a leader in areas of equal employment and safe workplace practices around the world. How do they support that standing? In ways that matter both to employees and customers.

For example, they were the first multinational apparel company to develop a comprehensive code of conduct designed to ensure that workers around the world making their products are safe and treated with dignity and respect. This helped set the stage for social responsibility when many other apparel providers were faced with detrimental backlash because of lagging workplace conditions. Which brings us to our next point.

Instead of solely focusing on the product, they innovate in their workplace practices to establish a desired image for their brand.

4. Ask yourself what you will have to *start doing, continue doing,* and *stop doing* to remain true to your passion and values.

If your passion and service are all about convenience and making it easy for your customers to do business, then what does that mean over time? What investments and checkpoints should be instituted into your processes to make them easier?

Make a list for your organization and make sure that every employee, especially managers, understands your commitment to it. This list should be a STOP, START, CONTINUE list. Populate this list with key activities that will be examined at regular intervals (maybe twice a year), and get all of your employees involved and enrolled.

To remain an integral part of their mass consumers' lifestyles, beverage companies had to stop myopically focusing on new derivatives of carbonated beverages and expand into new (and scary) territories. Sports beverages, energy beverages, water, and flavored water blends all started exploding, and the Coca-Colas and PepsiCo's of the world had to respond while continuing to remain true to the essence of their brands. Some endeavors were highly competitive, margin neutral, and not yet fully understood, so it had to be a journey that was taken carefully, in partnership and in passion with the customer.

5. Market from honesty and truth.

I got a call from a company recently. They left a message saying that they just wanted to call to "confirm my order." When I returned the call, I realized it was a ruse to try to get me to buy something new. They weren't confirming an order, and I felt I had been lied to when I called them back. If your company gets involved in this kind of deception, word will get out and customers will eventually steer clear of you. Don't believe that you have to lie to the customer to get their attention.

6. Make sure you have ongoing practices in place to involve and inspire your employees.

Ultimately your employees are your brand. They have to stay in touch with why we are doing these new things in the first place. Involve them in upgrades, revisions, and analyses of your business model. Reward them for getting it right. Employees are people, and people need recognition and support. They need to know that their work is meaningful and that if they jump on board with one of your new initiatives, they will share in the rewards down the line.

7. Remember that EVERYTHING speaks for your brand.

There are *things* such as your packaging, invoices, telephone answering system, Web site, signs, office environment, uniforms, vehicles, marketing collateral, and so on. And there are *methods:* color, font/type, verbiage or tone, texture, material, quality.

Do an audit a couple of times a year to sample all of the things that touch the customer and give them a score that tells the story of how well they adhere to your values and goals. When you pull together your audit, evaluate your efforts based on consistency and coherence. When I do this, I lay everything out together in a room—we call it the "war room"—and see how our world looks from our customer's point of view. After all, they are the last word in how successful your efforts have been.

8. Measure the changes that you are making and determine the following:

- What has worked: did you get what you were looking for?

- What isn't working: did you complete something but not get the return you were looking for?

- What hasn't been fulfilled: you never got to what you planned on doing?

9. Remember that it is a journey, and stay true to your purpose over time.

Remain tenacious and courageous in your quest for brand excellence. *Don't give up!* After a solid effort you'll find the ease that is realized when you are operating your business from a place of true meaning and authenticity, and getting there will be that much more energizing.

Even in the face of obstacles and adversity, the call for doing "what is right" for the brand and the customer will keep you grounded and confident in your convictions. It will bring about the change that keeps that emotional connection, the relationship that always wins over time.

Move Forward

I hope that the material in this book is as rewarding for you to implement as it was for me to write. Your brand and your passions can be one and the same, and the customer will respond to you if they are. Good luck and remember: always keep your marketing customer inspired!

About the Author

Aubyn Elaine Thomas

Aubyn Elaine Thomas has worked for some of the largest organizations in the world and is currently senior vice president of marketing services for Macy's. She has also held the position of vice president of the brand and acquisition for the marketing group of Harrah's Entertainment, Inc. and senior vice president of brand strategy and enterprise marketing for Bank of America. Her expertise includes credit and loyalty marketing, multicultural marketing, branding and acquisitions, brand strategy, and enterprise marketing. While managing billion-dollar brands, Ms. Thomas is also a motivational speaker and author.

Ms. Thomas holds two bachelor's degrees: one in mathematics from Spelman College, and one in electrical engineering from the Georgia Institute of Technology. She also holds an MBA in marketing from Clark Atlanta University. She lives in West Chester, Ohio.

www.ingramcontent.com/pod-product-compliance
Lightning Source LLC
Chambersburg PA
CBHW021952170526
45157CB00003B/955